British Railways Illustrated
SUMMER SPECIAL
No.4

IRWELL
PRESS

CONTENTS

SUBSCRIPTIONS

Readers can subscribe to British Railways Illustrated or its industrial/narrow gauge scion, Railway Bylines, for six or twelve issues at a time. The cost for six issues of BRILL is £15.00 inclusive of postage and packing whilst twelve issues are charged at £30.00. Bylines is bi-monthly and six issues for a year are £17.70 . Overseas subscribers should add the cost of surface/air mail. Limited numbers of back issues are also available. All remittances should be made out to IRWELL PRESS and sent to

Irwell Press General Office,
Mrs J. Gallagher,
P.O.Box 1260, Caernarfon, Gwynedd, LL55 3ZD
Telephone : 01286 871776
Fax : 01286 871605

Printed & Bound by Amadeus Press,
Huddersfield,
West Yorkshire

Cover. Waterloo, and off to the West Country with 35018 BRITISH INDIA LINE.

Right. 'I'd rather be on the beach!' Ladies working on steel reinforcing at Lowestoft Concrete Works, LNER, only a few yards from the sea, June 1943.

Frontispiece. The Brimscombe banker - an 0-6-2T at the rear of a freight climbing Sapperton. George Heiron.

Rear cover. Coronation Pacific No.46244 KING GEORGE VI about to depart Glasgow Central, August 1954. George Heiron.

Sand, Sun and... Beer

The truly great days of the railway Annual came in the late 1950s and early 1960s; diesels were an interesting if comfortably hypothetical concept and the best articles were concerned with *current* events on the railway. There were stirring tales of derring-do as Anointed Ones embarked on expeditions to the citadels of steam, apparently at the behest of the railway authorities, riding on locos to report back their findings to an astonished audience. Many such reports have, thirty years on and more, acquired the status of historical records in their own right. So, feeling the time to be ripe for a revival, we have persuaded R.C. Riley to update one of his famous reports - maybe with more to follow if they are as well-received as we expect. Beefed up additionally by a new set of photographs comes **A Night on the Beer, 1959.** Defy, if you can, the urge to quaff a pint or bottle after sampling the malt-heavy air of Burton on Trent, in the days when limitless casks were hauled about not by ghastly lorries but by the brewers' own saddle tanks.

Engine sheds, the natural homes of the steam locomotives and the places which haunt our dreams, have figured throughout the lifetime of *British Railways Illustrated*. They were the 'Cathedrals of Steam' indeed and lots of such fascinating, if conventional stuff, has long figured in the literature, with BRILL enjoying its share. There are many technical aspects, however, which are hardly ever touched upon and a timely little piece on an obscure shed, Kirkby-in-Ashfield, brings us once again, some thought provoking and unexpected insights. It was, **A Strange Transformation.**

It is not often appreciated that Britain probably enjoys more variation in its basic landscape (its geology, that is) than any other European country - or almost any country in the world for that matter. It is this underlying *variety* which provides the unique quality of some of our best lines, from the soft ice-laid clays of North Norfolk to the veritable Scandinavian coastline of Western Scotland. **The Kyle Line** was constructed through one of the finest products of our complex underlying geological history - wonderfully bleak and almost uninhabited terrain which retains much of its atmosphere today. The line was considered remarkable at the time, after all, for being '...the first railway passing through deer forests'.

Fourum comes in our *Specials* and *Annuals* in extra helpings and **Night and Day** is another familiar 'regular'. There are other, more general ingredients without which any self-respecting *Summer Special* could be regarded as incomplete. Such blooming perennials include the Somerset and Dorset; little excuse is needed for such familiar fare but another BRILL 'old stager' is *Station Survey* and here the two venerable institutions are married as one - **Station Survey, Evercreech Junction.** Summer shines from nearly every black and white page....

The best things come in twos and while not strictly a *Station Survey*, **Penzance: End of the Line** is near enough, with its detailed plan and thorough account. And what better place for a 'fifties summer than Land's End? That old bucket and spade feeling is nothing of course without the seaside and as a perfect balancing act to Penzance and Kyle there is (rocks again) that other glorious coast, a thorough contrast in every way - a different sea and different cliffs imparting a wholly different look to things. A different railway and different trains. **Along the North Yorkshire Coast** describes what is perhaps one of the greatest losses in the long sorrow of our railways; the exquisitely scenic, wild and windblown route from Teeside to Whitby and Scarborough must truly rank high in the scenery stakes. Built on the cheap and always strained by the peak time demands made on it, it was one of the few lines to have an *anemometer* wired to the signalling....

You'll Remember those Black & White Days...

Bass No.1 at Church Croft, 28th September 1957. Bass was the most rail-oriented of the Burton breweries and was the last to go over entirely to road transport. Photograph R.C. Riley.

A Night on the Beer
1959 classic, updated notes by R.C.Riley

'Caution! These gates will be opened when the bell rings,' In 1959 if you walked down any of the main streets of Burton on Trent you would come across this sign; and if you were one of the town's regular road users you would know that the bells rang many times each day. They were a warning that the gates were just about to *close*, for the sign referred to their opening for rail traffic. Soon a smartly groomed brewery engine would trundle wagons across the street from one part of the brewery to another; then the gates closed once more against rail traffic and passers by resumed their journeys. At one time there were twenty-seven such level crossings in Burton, many of them in everyday use.

Burton on Trent had several industries, but its was for its beer that the town was justly famed. The local well water had that quality that lends itself to the brewing of good beer and this had been Burton's principal activity for some 200 years. At the turn of the century there were some forty firms connected with the brewing industry, but even by the late 1950s the number had been substantially depleted as a result of amalgamations. Of the handful of large breweries remaining, four had their own railway systems and locomotives to operate them.

The main line reached Burton as early as 1839, in the form of the Birmingham & Derby Junction Railway. In 1844 this company was acquired by the Midland Railway, which enjoyed a monopoly of most of the local traffic for nearly twenty years. Inevitably, other companies turned covetous eyes towards this source of revenue but it was the Midland Railway Acts of 1859 and 1860 that first provided railway access into the breweries themselves. Prior to that beer had been despatched from the breweries in horse-drawn carts and often long strings of them awaiting access to the station brought all other traffic to a standstill. It was this state of affairs that ensured Parliamentary approval for the Acts, overcoming considerable local opposition to the proposed street level crossings - on the grounds that they would alleviate the chaotic traffic situation then existing. In 1861, before these branches had been opened, the LNWR gained access to Burton and, as might be expect, there were many disputes between the two companies before they settled down to share the traffic tolerantly, if not amicably.

Towards the end of 1862, the Guild Street branch was opened, serving, among others, the three premises of Messrs. Bass, Worthington and Allsop. At first the branch was worked partly by engines and partly by horses provided by the Midland Railway but in 1863 Bass acquired its first engine. One by one the other breweries in Burton followed suit. The Hay branch, partly opened in 1861, was completed throughout three years later. The Burton railway map was considerably augmented by the opening of other lines, notably the Horninglow and Shobnall branches in 1873, the Bond End branch in 1874 and the LNWR Dallow Lane branch in 1882. In 1848 the North Staffordshire Railway had started running freight trains into Burton; thirty years later the Great Northern arrived on the scene. The early branches were the property of the Midland, which zealously guarded its rights, but over the years it had gradually to surrender its monopoly and allow the other companies access to them.

By 1959 the most extensive of Burton's brewery rail systems was that of Messrs. Bass and Worthington, who had 16 miles of their own track and running powers over a further 10 miles of BR metals. It was not always easy to see where BR ended and the Bass-Worthington territory began, as the lines were worked only by the brewery engines. With the large numbers of level crossings there was an equally

Bass No.1 (the engine was scrapped in 1963) on 30th May 1960 in the Middle Brewery triangle, between Allsopp's Crossing and Guild Street Crossing - the saloon, now preserved in the Bass Museum, was kept in the shed at the right. Photograph R.C. Riley.

large number of signalboxes, but most of these were operated by BR personnel. The usual bell system was employed for the acceptance of trains and the long single-line section from Wellington Street Junction to Shobnall Maltings was controlled by Tyers to-ken instruments. On the privately owned portion of the system there was a whistle code by which the engine driver notified the signalman of his intentions - for example, which track he wished to enter or if he was going over a crossing in order to shunt back into another line. On all such occasions a shunter accompanied the train. Two types of signal were in use - ordinary semaphore arms and some revolving crossbar arms, strange sights to modern eyes; one of these signals protected the line at Allsops

Bass No.9 (now preserved at the Bass museum) on 28th September 1957. It was a Thornewill and Warham - the local Burton builders - engine and was notable for having hauled the saloon for King Edward VIII on 22nd May 1902. Photograph R.C. Riley.

Crossing, where the Ind Coope system crossed the Bass system on the level. The operating staff worked on a double shift basis.

To operate such an extensive system a large fleet of locomotives was necessary. In 1959 the Bass stock consisted of eight steam and four diesel, and the Worthington stock three steam and six diesel locomotives. Of this total of twenty-one, up to sixteen engines were in use daily. The Bass engines were in a pleasant red livery, officially designated Turkey Red. Two were normally spare, one for boiler washout and one for major repairs, carried out in the company's own workshops. The oldest steam engines in service were Nos.3 and 7, two 0-4-0 saddle tanks built by the local firm of Thornewill & Warham in 1890 and 1875 respectively. These were distinctive for their 4ft driving wheels; their cylinders were 14in by 20in and boiler pressure 120lb. The other steam engines were similar in appearance, but apart from 3ft 6in wheels they were slightly larger dimensionally. They comprised Nos.1, 2, 9, 10 and 11 (built by Neilson in 1899-1901) and No.4 built by the North British Locomotive Co. in 1912. As the steam engines wore out they were replaced by diesels but the former were in such good condition that the process was a gradual one. The diesel fleet consisted of Nos.5 (80 hp) and 6 (200 hp) built by the local firm of Baguley in 1939 and 1958 respectively; No.8, a Ruston of 1957 in dark blue livery, and No.12 (207 hp) a 1959 Sentinel-built machine with a Rolls-Royce engine.

The Worthington engines were equally well kept, but in blue livery. Their steam engines were also of the 0-4-0 saddle tank type - Nos.2, 4 and

6 built by Hudswell Clarke in 1904, 1901 and 1920; and the larger Nos.1 and 5 built by Bagnall in 1945 and 1923 respectively. The six diesels were small 40 hp Simplex-type vehicles built between 1924 and 1934, some of which originally had petrol engines.

The Ind Coope system was mostly confined within the brewery limits and so it was less elaborately signalled. It had five engines which were kept in a shed not far from the former LNWR motive power depot at Horninglow Bridge. There were two Baguley diesels, built in 1951-52, two 'Super-Sentinel' steam locomotives, built in 1947-48 and a battery electric locomotive, built for the War Department in 1922 and acquired in 1946. These engines were all in olive green livery. The Ind Coope maltings at Shobnall were shunted by BR locomotives.

Truman, Hanbury Buxton & Co. Ltd had one engine, a green Peckett 0-4-0 saddle tank of 1949 vintage which only operated as far as the BR transfer sidings adjacent to the brewery. The fourth brewery with its own locomotives was that of Marston, Thompson & Evershed Ltd. Their steam engine, a Hawthorn Leslie 0-4-0 saddle tank of 1924, was normally kept spare and most of the work was done by a 1955 Baguley diesel, which worked over BR tracks as far as Shobnall sidings.

British Railways engines for handling the beer traffic were mostly supplied by the former Midland Railway shed at Burton, close to the main line near Leicester Junction. At the time of my visit the largest engines allocated were fifteen Crab 2-6-0s, five of which were fitted with Reidinger poppet-valve gear. They were also used

Above: No.3 (a Thornewill and Warham engine of the early 1890s) at the Bass shed, 30th May 1960. The precipitous decline of the Burton beer traffic is often laid directly at the door of the 1955 ASLEF strike. It certainly highlighted the brewer's vulnerability to disruption in rail traffic (to their considerable consternation) and in the book *Brewery Railways* (D&C 1985) Ian P. Peaty relates that the threat of a further strike 'caused near panic' - Bass' symbolic response was to pull down the brewery entrance gates to allow in articulated lorries! Photograph R.C. Riley.

Bass No.3, 30th May 1960. Photograph R.C. Riley.

Right: Bass No.1, with the little shed beyond, about to cross Guild Street on 30th May 1960. There were actually two sheds, both of two roads, in the triangle at the Middle Brewery - the other lies out of sight to the left. Photograph R.C. Riley.

Worthington No.5 at Hawkins Lane, 26th May 1959. Photograph R.C. Riley.

on passenger work, especially in the summer months. Burton also had twenty five 4F and five 3F 0-6-0s, but the latter were confined to local trip work and shunting duties.

Yard shunting at Burton was carried out entirely by former Midland Railway 0-6-0s of Classes 2F 3F and 4F, with some assistance from standard 3F tanks. The individual duties of the engines were clearly defined and could readily be identified by the tar-

get numbers carried. The shunting duties were taken over progressively by 350hp diesel shunters early in 1959, when three were introduced in the Dixie, Horninglow and Leicester Junction yards; later there were nine of them at Burton to cover eight duties. They were fuelled and maintained at Derby, changing over each week. Eventually a small diesel was allocated to cover duties over the Shobnall and Bond End branches, then performed

by former MR 0-4-0 tanks of Deeley design, which were the largest engines permitted over some of the sharp curves of the Bond End line; two of this type, Nos.41532 and 41536 were at Burton for this duty, and in 1959 the complement still included four Class 3F 0-6-0 tanks, employed on shunting work.

The layout of the various yards at Burton was rather complicated and the general pattern of freight traffic

Worthington No.1, 12th May 1958. Worthington also had several petrol engine locos, converted to diesel in the 1950s - one stands beyond at the platform. Photograph R.C. Riley.

Worthington No.12, again with that glorious cab plate, 28th September 1957. Allsopp's Crossing box stands beyond. Photograph R.C. Riley.

had changed little since 1923. Thus GN section trains still used Hawkins Lane, those of the one-time NSR system used New Dixie and those to and from former LNWR destinations were accommodated in Horninglow yard, close to the ex-LNWR engine shed. The Midland Railway, of course, was the senior partner in Burton and the majority of traffic was made up of trains using former MR lines. Most through freight trains which called to pick up or set down traffic at Burton used

Wetmore sidings, which were also the starting point for many northbound trains. Southbound trains started from Horninglow Bridge yard - notably for Birmingham, Bristol and London. So many freight trains conveyed beer traffic partly or wholly, and not all of these originated from Burton. In the years up until 1959 there had been considerable progress in the fitting of vacuum brakes to freight wagons and by that year fitted wagons only were used for the beer traffic.

Loading of wagons was carried out inside the individual breweries by their own employees. Each brewery might have had several different loading points and, particularly in the case of the Bass-Worthington system, they could be widely scattered. It was at one of the Bass loading points that I watched this work during my visit to Burton. There, in warehouses or on loading bays, were barrels and barrels of beer - at least that was what I thought at first, but my impressions

Worthington No.4 on 28th September 1957. Photograph R.C. Riley.

Truman Hanbury and Buxton's Peckett, works number 2136 of 1953, on 12th April 1958. Photograph R.C. Riley.

were soon corrected. A barrel holds 36 gallons; to more knowledgeable eyes than mine, the other casks were either pins (4.5 gallons), firkins (9 gallons), kilderkins (18 gallons), hogsheads (54 gallons), or butts (108 gallons). At some loading banks rollerways were provided to ease the work but at Shobnall the job was carried out no differently from, and probably just as quickly, as it had when the brewery first opened. Each loader had a 'bobbing stick' slightly longer than a walking stick, with which he trundled casks unerringly on to the loading bay and up the ramp into the wagon, not once touching them with his hands. By this means some forty wagons were loaded at Shobnall that day. The previous day, a Monday, no fewer than ninety five wagons had been loaded there. The total capacity of a covered wagon amounted to about 20 hogsheads, standing upright, while an open wagon would take 60 firkins.

The beer store at Shobnall was a large building, on each side of which lay long loading banks. As the loading of each wagon was completed according to its manifest, the open vehicles had their loads made secure. In warm weather a Bass engine collected the loaded wagons and hauled then up and down beneath a cold water spray, a process known as 'spargeing' which helped to ensure that the beer left the brewery in the best possible condition. Then the Bass engine moved its load into the LMR transfer sidings, from which the wagons were tripped to the sorting sidings to be made up into

trains for their respective destinations.

Beer of course, formed a substantial portion of Burton's total freight traffic. In a typical week in May 1959, just before my visit, the 3,770 wagons forwarded from the town comprised 1,522 of beer, 2,166 of general merchandise and 82 of coal and minerals. This figure included transfer traffic not originating at Burton. With a turnover of this magnitude, there had to be careful supervision of wagon availability.

In practice the supply of empties presented little difficulty because the majority were provided from loaded wagons working into the breweries with empty casks, hops or barley. In addition, the sidings at Burton had four roads capable of stabling 200 empty wagons and as far as possible these were kept fully occupied, not only to meet normal day to day requirements but also the ever-present possibility of emergency demand. When the number of empties available fell below a certain level a train of them was ordered from Control. Often these came from Chaddesden sidings, Derby, in which case they included a proportion of repaired wagons from the workshops. Burton on Trent in 1959 had an allocation of about 700 shock absorbing wagons which were employed solely on beer traffic, running outwards with beer and returning with empty casks.

In addition to the open and covered goods wagons normally used for beer traffic some special wagons were

used for subsidiary products - notably, bulk grain wagons for barley and malt. During the winter months Burton handled some 70,000 tons of barley for the breweries, most of it from the Eastern Counties, with some from the South and the Midlands. After the barley had been through the maltings some of it was despatched elsewhere, Ind Coope for example sending a few thousand tons of malt each year to its subsidiary in Alloa, Scotland and in return receiving a considerable tank wagon traffic of lager, for bottling. This bottling ale, incidentally, was of special importance for it had to be dealt with within a few hours and hence next-day delivery had to be guaranteed. Bass also had some tank wagon traffic, mostly destined for Ireland, via Heysham or Holyhead, for Termonde in Belgium via Harwich and for the Channel Islands. The wagons themselves were railway owned, but the cylindrical tanks were painted in individual brewery colours and lifted off by crane for dispatch to their destination by road. The tanks contained the equivalent of thirty barrels of beer. Other subsidiary traffic included the spent hops sent away as fertiliser and the wet grain used in the manufacture of cattle feed.

Train loads fluctuated according to seasonal demand, but generally speaking were heavier at the beginning of each week as the pubs and clubs replenished their stocks after heavy weekend drinking. Whit Monday 1959 was an example of such fluctuations - the weekend was mainly warm and dry and it was the first Bank Holiday to follow the Chancellor's concession of 2d off a pint. No train was scheduled to run on the Monday but London did such a roaring trade that at short notice a special thirty six wagon train was put on. Both in the breweries and the transfer sidings staff had always to be standing by, to deal with just such a situation.

Before making a journey north on one of the beer trains, I spent some time observing the workings of the Burton yards. Walking northwards from Burton station, the first yard I reached was Horninglow Bridge, where a 3F 0-6-0 was busily marshalling the 6.50pm train for St. Pancras. The engine for the St. Pancras beer train was a Crab 2-6-0 which left a few minutes before time with a load of thirty four wagons. At Hawkins Lane another 3F 0-6-0 was preparing the three evening departures over the GN line so keenly that the trains were ready well before time. The 6.15pm York left at 5.56pm and the 6.55pm Colwick at 6.29pm, both with K3 2-6-0s in charge. Shortly after the latter departure a B1 4-6-0 running tender first brought in a heavy freight from the GN line, including a large proportion of empty shock-absorbing wagons. Although the loads were not heavy, the K3s made spectacular starts, for there was a sustained climb out of Hawkins Lane before the flyover which carried the GN route over the main line.

A diesel was shunting Old Dixie yard, while 0-6-0T No.47643 was forming an up train for a transfer trip to Wetmore sidings. At 6.15pm No.5 one of the sturdy little Bagnall tanks in the Worthington fleet emerged from the brewery sidings past Horninglow shed and Hawkins Lane to deposit a load of twenty-two wagons in Old Dixie sidings. As soon as it returned to the brewery a bevy of BR engines arrived to divide the load between them, No.43679 taking some wagons to Hawkins Lane for GN destinations and No.44420 moving others away to Horninglow Bridge, while No.47643 added the remainder to its rake of wagons for Wetmore sidings.

Soon after 7pm 4F 0-6-0 No.44245 passed by on the main line with a load of nine wagons and a brake from Shobnall bound for Wetmore sidings, there to form the 8.25pm train to Carlisle, on which I was to make a journey north. It was followed by 3F 0-6-0T No.47643 with fifteen wagons on a transfer trip from Old Dixie to Wetmore.

All northbound traffic for Midland line destinations was marshalled at Wetmore sidings. There were thirteen roads in all and on four of these were standing the wagons to form the 8.25pm train. These four contained, respectively, the traffic for Rotherham, Masborough, Leeds, Skipton and Scotland, and the wagons were attached to the engine in that order. As I ar-

rived the 0-6-0 tank was quickly disposing of its beer wagons from Dixie in the appropriate sidings, after which the 4F started making up its train.

At 7.17pm the 5.10pm Birmingham Rowsley freight was due, but it was delayed by a late-running northbound express, and it was not until after 7.30pm that a Crab Mogul backed it into the sidings. This train took beer traffic for Blackburn, Burnley, Bury, Rochdale and Manchester and was due to leave in the wake of the 2.55pm Bristol Dringhouses fast freight which passed through behind a 9F 2-10-0. After the Rowsley freight and the 5pm Bristol-York passenger, due to leave Burton at 8.05pm, there were no scheduled trains over the road before the Carlisle freight.

By this time the Carlisle train had been fully marshalled and now consisted of twenty-two wagons and a brakevan. Eight of these wagons contained transfer traffic from points other than Burton but the remaining fourteen were all of Burton beer, and were destined as follows: five for Barrow-in-Furness; one each for Ulverston, Kendal, Leeds and Dewsbury; two for Appleby; two for Glasgow; and one for Aberdeen. Much of the Scottish traffic had been taken the previous evening on the Mondays only 9.10pm Niddrie freight, a load of nineteen wagons hauled by a Crab.

The York passenger left on time and 4F 0-6-0 No.44245 had a clear

3F tank No.47464 shunts Wetmore Sidings on 26th May 1959. Photograph R.C. Riley.

41536 on the main line at Shobnall, 30th May 1960. The little MR tanks derived a wide versatility from their light weight and tiny wheelbase and were retained for the tightly curved Shobnall and Bond End branches. M.F. Higson, in his *London Midland Fireman* (Ian Allan 1972) could not wait to end the Burton phase of his career (abiding memory the smell of malt) and grimly describes the little 0-4-0Ts as 'very comfortless'. Free cans of ale on some of the shunts seem to have been the only consolation. Photograph R.C. Riley.

road. I had not expected such humble motive power and in fact the train was diagrammed for a Burton Class 5, normally a Crab (the diagram was later altered and a Saltley Class 5 4-6-0 provided). 4F engines were not permitted to work Class C fully fitted freight trains so we were reduced in status to a partly fitted train, with Class D headlamps. As the load consisted only of twenty-three wagons the 0-6-0 had

an easy task (the previous evening another 4F had been turned out to work the maximum load for its type - forty-three wagons). Driver A. Wright of Burton assured me that even with the full load a 4F 0-6-0 in good condition could maintain the relatively easy schedule, and so it proved.

About three minutes before time we had the road and No.44245 edged gently out of the sidings on to

the goods loop, in contrast to the spirited effort of B1 No.61141 which I could see vigorously tackling the sharp climb to the bridge over the main line with the 8.30pm freight for Colwick as we approached. At Clay Mills Junction we crossed to the main line and after recovering from a signal check at Stenson Junction speed rose to a steady 36mph until the outskirts of Derby. Derby station was relatively

Crab 42900 heads the 5.15pm Birmingham - Rowsley freight at Burton, 26th May 1959. Photograph R.C. Riley.

quiet at this time of the evening, but I was denied the unfamiliar experience of passing through without stopping, as we were brought to a brief stand while a diesel railcar made a shunting movement. Once more No.44245 made a gentle start and it was not until we passed Derby North Junction that the engine was opened up in readiness for the sustained climb ahead. As we passed Belper there was a glimpse of the River Derwent and soon the full beauty of this part of Derbyshire was apparent. We plodded on at 36mph past Ambergate Junction where the Manchester line diverges and the disused North Midland station building of 1840 stood as a monument to the fine railway architecture of those days, although it was later

Breaking & Dismantling Co. and the coaches in question had been sold for scrap. At Tapton Junction, where the Sheffield line diverges, No.44245 was maintaining a gallant 45mph and we were still ahead of time. Near Barrow Hill Junction No.92167 one of the mechanical stoker-fitted 2-10-0s, made an impressive sight on another fast freight, the 4.03pm Carlisle - Birmingham.

Staveley shed was the scene of great activity as were the various collieries we passed over the next few miles. This section of line was subject to numerous speed restrictions, usually 20mph, as a result of colliery subsidence. Furthermore our progress was hampered by signal checks, and no sooner was No.44245 opened up

eight wagons of our load and to add nineteen more. There was much of interest to be seen here, including two express trains bound for Bristol, one from Newcastle in the charge of a V2 2-6-2 and one from Bradford with a Jubilee. As soon as these trains had gone on their way attention was focused on the south end of the station for the passage of the down 'Condor' express freight from London to Glasgow, running dead on time with two 1,200hp Metrovick diesels in command. In contrast to this outstanding development in modern freight train running (as we saw it then) was the Rotherham Masborough yard pilot, simmering gently in the moonlight - a Midland 0-6-0T No.41835 just repainted and still essentially in its

42763 on the 6.50pm St Pancras, 26th May 1959. This was the engine referred to in the text; a 3F 0-6-0 had busily marshalled the train, the Crab leaving a few minutes before time with a load of thirty four wagons. Photograph R.C. Riley.

demolished At Crich Junction the gradient sharpened and No.44245 was opened out in earnest until the summit was reached at Stretton. We had now been on our way for an hour and in spite of two signal checks were running slightly ahead of schedule. At Clay Cross in the gathering dusk, a Caprotti Class 5 4-6-0 passed working hard up-grade with the 6.45pm fast freight from Bradford to St. Pancras.

Beyond Chesterfield we passed sidings containing several long rakes of WR coaches. I was only too well aware that the Western Region's summer service depended to no small extent on a plentiful supply of LMR coaches, but this was the first indication that I had seen of the existence of a two-way traffic! I soon had the explanation, though, for the sidings were those of the Chesterfield Steel

after a slack than adverse signals were sighted and the regulator had to be shut again. At Woodhouse Mill we passed through one of the vast steelworks for which Sheffield was renowned.

The Sheffield District line diverged at Treeton Junction where too was Canklow shed, to which No.44245 was allocated. Soon after this we entered Masborough Sorting Sidings where an 8-minute stop was scheduled for the engine to take water. In fact our small tendered engine needed only 6 minutes and we were soon on our way again for the short run to Rotherham Masborough, where we set back into the sidings. Signal checks had cost us 5 minutes but as 40 minutes were allowed to remarshal the train there was an ample recovery margin. It did not take long to shed

1892 condition, with open cab and spring-balance safety valves on the dome.

As 11pm we resumed our journey with the load increased to thirty-four wagons. The little Barclay 0-4-0 saddle tanks were busy at the vast Park Gate Iron & Steel Co. works outside Rotherham where the furnaces lit the night sky. Beyond Swinton Junction the lights of the much-modernised Manvers Main Colliery could be seen for some miles. Here too there was considerably activity and some modern Hunslet 0-6-0 saddle tanks were at work. Our route was still subject to several speed restrictions and by the time we had passed the last of them at Normanton we were running 15 minutes late, in spite of a 43mph maximum on the level stretch at Darfield. Normanton shed provided the

4F No.44420 in Dixie Sidings, 26th May 1959. These sidings lay to the north of the station, close to North Stafford Junction, between the Hay Street and Guild Street branches - there were six principal branches serving the breweries and associated buildings, named after the streets most closely associated with each district. Photograph R.C. Riley.

contrast of MR 0-6-0s standing cheek-by-jowl with NER 0-6-0 tanks. From here on the road was anything but clear and after several signal stops we entered Hunslet yard at 12.40am, over half an hour late. None of this time could be charged to No.44245 which had given a good account of itself throughout the journey and now came off the train to run light to Holbeck. In contrast to out lateness the up 'Condor' express freight passed

through exactly on time. This was remarkable when the later history of the Metrovick Co-Bo diesels is considered.

While a diesel engine was marshalling the train I was enjoying a welcome cup of tea in the Yardmaster's office. There I learnt that Hunslet sidings dealt with some 3,500 wagons each day, and that the beer on my train would now take second place to a greater proportion of West Riding woollen traffic. Much of this came off the

9.40pm freight from Healey Mills which brought traffic from such places as Sowerby Bridge, Cleckheaton and Halifax. The load too was likely to include agricultural machinery and confectionery. Departure from Hunslet Yard was scheduled for 1.30am and several minutes before this Inspector Willis entered the office and eyed me with evident relief; "I was beginning to wonder if ye'd no' turned up", he explained, and went on to tell me that

Burton on 26th May 1959, and 3F 0-6-0 No.43679 shunts Wetmore (could there be a more appropriate name, in Burton of all places?) Sidings. 43679 figures in the text, emerging to help take up the load at Old Dixie, and hauling some wagons off to Hawkins Lane for GN destinations. Photograph R.C. Riley.

he was from Carlisle Kingmoor shed, as were the crew, Driver Wilson and Fireman Macdonald. This was a lodging turn and they had brought down the 5.30pm fitted freight from Carlisle Durran Hill the previous evening. Although our train was rostered for a Leeds engine it was often used for engines from northern sheds which had worked south with no balanced return working, so it was that our engine, too, came from Carlisle Kingmoor - Class 5 2-6-0 No.42835.

The train was now running fully fitted and made up to a load of forty five wagons. I have always regarded the Fowler Crabs as rather cumbersome machines but the appearance of an engine was nothing to go by and No.42835 certainly proved master of

was clear as we passed Whitehall Junction where the passenger lines out of Leeds City rejoin the main line and at this point No.42835 was opened up for the first time. In the suburbs between Armley and Kirkstall there was a brief stretch of falling gradient and we took full advantage of this in readiness for the long climb ahead.

There was no respite for the fireman at this stage, for when he was not firing he had to use the pricker to get the fire into good shape. Fortunately the worst part of this climb was over by the time we sighted adverse signals after Thackley Tunnel and three signal stops followed on the outskirts of Shipley. Late running of a passenger train from Bradford was to blame and the delays cost 20 min-

A relaying slack at Settle on the 1 in 100 climb brought our speed down to 15mph and in recovering from this setback our thunderous assault on the Pennines really began. It was the fireman's conviction that regular use of the fire irons was essential to enable a Crab to maintain steam on the long banks. He did this with such good effect that No.42835 never faltered, and we seemed even to be holding our own with the down sleeper, for another adverse distant was sighted before Horton-in-Ribblesdale. In spite of the checks we maintained the booked time from Skipton and so were comfortably tucked away in the loop line at Blea Moor before the 9.15pm. St. Pancras - Glasgow was due to pass. A friendly glimmer of light in the signalbox was

2F 0-6-0 No.58128 at Burton, and soon to be withdrawn, 28th September 1957. Photograph R.C. Riley.

its job. The high cab contrasted strongly to that of the 4F 0-6-0 but the engine did not ride as well. We pulled out of Hunslet sidings on time at 1.30am but experience had evidently taught Driver Wilson that there was no point in opening up until he had passed the centre of Leeds. As we made our way slowly along the goods road we passed a stationary passenger train on the adjacent main line. It was the 7.45pm Marylebone - Glasgow 'Starlight Special' and its Jubilee was taking water. This train overtook us as we approached Holbeck shed and was no doubt responsible for the signal checks that ensued. These did not bring us to a stand for the driver had things judged to a nicety and we continued our unhurried progress through the sleeping city. The road

utes in all, although this could easily be recovered as a 32 minute stop was scheduled at Skipton South Junction. This was to enable the engine to take water and also to allow the 9pm St. Pancras - Edinburgh to pass. The express was running 12 minutes late that night with 'Royal Scot' No.46113 CAMERONIAN in charge. It was inevitable, therefore, that our departure from Skipton was late and we started so promptly in the wake of the express that we were checked by distant signals out to Hellifield and were unable to take advantage of the favourable gradient before the 15 mile 'Long Drag' from Settle Junction to Blea Moor. Settle Junction was passed 10 minutes late at 3.34am by which time it had become sufficiently light to identify the passing mile posts.

the only sign of life in that desolate moorland outpost. There was plenty of time to take water, for Britannia Pacific No.70054 DORNOCH FIRTH was a few minutes late with the down express.

Hardly had its tail light disappeared amid a swirl of smoke in Blea Moor tunnel than the road was set for us to draw out of the loop and before we reached the main line signal it came off. A certain amount of slipping was unavoidable in the damp fastness of the tunnel and it took 4 minutes 30 seconds to thread its 2,629 yards length. Then the hard work was over and as we passed Ais Gill Summit the regulator was shut, the driver's hand moving to the brake valve in order to keep speed within the prescribed limit of 55mph for Class C freight trains.

Horninglow Yard on 26th May 1959. The old LNW shed, empty (as it so often was by this time) in this view, was an oddity; it had long operated more or less as a stabling point and the LMS had rebuilt it with a new roof, only for the allocation to more or less fade away within a few years. Photograph R.C. Riley.

We were now treated to the sight of a procession of up freights relentlessly hammering their way up the bank, emphasising the importance of the Settle - Carlisle route as a freight traffic artery at that time. At Appleby smart work enabled us to leave two wagons of beer in less than half the time allowed, so that we came to the end of our journey in the yard at Carlisle Petteril Bridge dead on time at 6.10am.

As at Burton-on-Trent the railway geography of Carlisle had altered but little since the 1923 Grouping. Eight railway companies used to serve Carlisle and their seven individual goods yards all survived, although an extensive reorganisation scheme was well under way in which traffic would largely be concentrated in the new yard at Kingmoor. My train was worked forward either to Viaduct Yard (ex-Caledonian) or to London Road (ex-North Eastern). Beer for the State-owned pubs of Carlisle was then worked by trip train to Dentonholme goods depot (ex-GSWR) from where road deliv-

Close by the LNW Horninglow shed, at the Allsopp's Cooperage, lay another shed, a two road building which was home to the company's mixed bag of locos. Allsopp amalgamated with Ind Coope back in the 1930s to give Ind, Coope and Allsopp but the ancient name (which gave us India Pale Ale according to legend) was dispensed with in 1959, leaving the more prosaic Ind Coope. Locos here on 28th September 1957 are Sentinels 7 and 8, and English Electric No.9. Photograph R.C. Riley.

44245 prepares for its Night on the Beer, with the 8.25pm for Carlisle (it came off at Leeds, as the text relates) at Burton on 26th May 1959. Photograph R.C. Riley.

ery services took over. Scottish traffic went to Kingmoor for GSWR destinations or to Canal Yard for those on the former NBR line.

Bulk deliveries of beer to Carlisle took place only once a week, usually on Mondays, when the 9.10 Burton - Niddrie relieved the 8.25pm of much of the Scottish traffic. I visited Dentonholme early on a Wednesday morning to find that the whole of the previous day's consignment had been unloaded and most of it already delivered to replenish stocks in the local hostelries. There were still a few casks for road delivery that morning. They bore labels with the name of the dispatching brewery in Burton and that of the landlord of the house to which

they were addressed *The Royal Scot*, *The Red Lion* and so on. Although I had not accompanied those particular casks north I felt a strong proprietary interest in them and as I sank a pint in the local that evening I offered silent thanks to the 8.25pm and my night on the beer.

Postscript

The speed of the rundown of beer traffic was remarkable. In early 1960 Messrs. Bass and Worthington combined their business and the latter engines were renumbered into the Bass fleet. In the same year the total rundown of the system began, with beer being pumped to a loading point in

the Middle Brewery. The Bass engine shed closed in 1966 and remaining engines transferred to the Worthington shed but rail traffic ceased altogether the following year. Bass No.9 and the four wheel saloon were retained as part of a new Bass Museum. Rail traffic at Marstons and Trumans also ceased in the mid-1960s, while that of Ind Coope survived only until 1970.

The original version of this text was published in Trains Illustrated Annual 1962, *and the kind co-operation of the publisher, Ian Allan, is gratefully acknowledged.*

End of the road. Some of the local Crab 2-6-0s at Carlisle Kingmoor, 29 May 1959. Photograph R.C. Riley.

Many railway photographers sought a suitable 'frame' for their pictures - signals often figured but perhaps the most convenient proved to be the bridge arch. By this device a different kind of 'inside looking out' effect was achieved, an almost private, intimate way of depicting an otherwise ordinary train. These four fine efforts by *John Scrace* are classic essays in the craft, all taken on the Southern Region in the 1960s. Above is BR 2-6-4T No.80147 on the 1.05pm Wareham to Swanage, at Worgret Junction on 8th June 1964 and below, Pacific 34022 EXMOOR on the 11.30am Waterloo - Bournemouth West train at Swanwick (diverted via Fareham through engineering work), on 25th April 1965.

More 'through the arches' with (above) 34026 YES TOR on the down Bournemouth Belle in Clapham Cutting on 4th June 1966 and below, another 2-6-4T, 80144, on the 4.47pm Tunbridge Wells West to Three Bridges, at Worth on 10th May 1965. All photographs John Scrace.

Station Survey

On 7 August 1965 - the last summer of operations on the S&D - the 4.20pm Templecombe-Bath service was handled by 2-6-4T No.80037, seen here taking on water at Evercreech Junction. Meanwhile, Ivatt 2-6-2T No.41291 stands on the middle road - when the Bath train has departed and cleared the section, it will back into the platform to work the 5.00pm to Highbridge. Both engines display the 83G shedplates of Templecombe. Photograph Hugh Ballantyne.

EVERCREECH JUNCTION

By Oliver Maitland

The name of Evercreech Junction trips readily off the tongues of railway enthusiasts who have never even set foot in the county of Somerset - evidence, as if it were needed, of the celebrity status of, not only the much-missed Somerset & Dorset line, but also what was, arguably, one of Britain's most notable rural junctions. However, the station, like the line on which it stood, failed to maintain a similar renown among the general travelling public (the Western Region of British Railways not exactly helping in that matter); the inevitable outcome was its appearance on that seemingly endless list of mid-1960s closures.

Evercreech did not start life as a junction, nor was it born as part of the legendary Somerset & Dorset Railway. In August 1854 a line between Highbridge and Glastonbury was opened by the Somerset Central Railway, and by March 1859 the line had been extended at both ends - to

Burnham in the west and to Wells in the east. Meanwhile, a line threading northwards from Wimborne (near Bournemouth) was under construction, albeit rather slowly, by the Dorset Central Railway, and the two independent companies - the Somerset Central and the Dorset Central - later agreed to collaborate in order to complete a new cross-country line between Burnham and Poole, one of the aims being to provide a connection between ports on the Bristol Channel and the English Channel. The Somerset Central's contribution to the new through route necessitated an extension from Glastonbury to Cole, at which latter point the Dorset Central would be met end-on.

The Glastonbury - Cole section - complete with Evercreech station, a mile or so to the south of the village it nominally served - was deemed ready for the obligatory Board of Trade inspection in January 1862, Colonel Yolland doing the honours: *'...laid single throughout, with sidings at the Stations at West Pennard, Pylle and*

Evercreech ...land has been purchased and the works constructed for a double line...'. Col. Yolland was satisfied with most of the works, but required that the arrangements at Wells Junction (where the new line joined the original one) be revised before he could sanction the opening of the line to public traffic. The SCR, undeterred, carried out its ceremonial opening of the new line on 18 January 1862, but it was 3 February before public traffic could be accommodated.

The whole of the new line was laid with mixed gauge rails, although the mixing of the gauges was, it seems, not actually completed until 3 February. The requirement for mixed gauge rails was due to the existing SCR lines having originally been worked by the broad gauge Bristol & Exeter Railway, whereas the new line was intended to connect with the Dorset Central, a standard gauge concern. (It was not only the new line on which the gauge was mixed - the *whole* of the SCR had been mixed by 3 February 1862). Regarding gauges, the SCR

had undergone a transitional phase - the working agreement with the B&ER had expired on 28 August 1861, and the SCR subsequently worked its own services with broad gauge locomotives borrowed from the B&ER. It was 3 February 1862 when the SCR started working its own lines with its own standard gauge engines. The broad gauge rails at Evercreech were not, however, wholly superfluous - until *circa* 1864 a broad gauge B&E goods train occasionally worked through from Glastonbury to Evercreech. One consequence of the line through Evercreech station having been engineered to accommodate the broad gauge was that there was a very generous space between the two platforms - something commonplace on broad gauge lines, but not usually associated with what later became the Somerset & Dorset.

As for the through route between Burnham and Poole, it wasn't finished until August 1863. By that time the Somerset Central and the Dorset Central Railways had merged to become the Somerset & Dorset Railway.

From Evercreech to the North

The S&D started life in poor financial health. Although it operated at a nominal profit, the income was woefully inadequate to foot all the bills, let alone pay interest on capital and dividends to shareholders, and the company subsequently spent several years in the hands of Receivers. In 1871, after its release from receiver-

ship, the S&D embarked on a 'do or die' mission. This took the form of the celebrated extension over the Mendip Hills via the North Somerset coalfield to Bath, where a potentially valuable connection would be made with the recently arrived Midland Railway. The Bath extension, across some exceedingly difficult terrain, including the summit at Masbury, 811 feet above sea level - was constructed very swiftly, less than three years elapsing between authorisation (21 August 1871) and opening (20 July 1874). The Bath extension joined the original Somerset Central (Burnham - Poole) line a little under half a mile to the north-west of Evercreech station, the station thereby becoming a junction, and retitled accordingly. On the extension itself, a station was provided nearer to the village of Evercreech - named Evercreech New, it was just over a mile along the line from Evercreech Junction. The Bath extension was an extremely bold venture, but it proved to be the pecuniary straw which broke the camel's back. The S&D's financial salvation came in the form of a joint lease by the Midland and the LSWR, the lease being agreed in November 1875.

Prior to the opening of the Bath extension the line was inspected for the Board of Trade by Colonel Rich, a series of examinations of which two extended over four days. Among the more straightforward matters was an entry in the report of 21 June 1874: '...second platforms with shelter for the

Rural delight - 4MT 2-6-4T No.80037 pulls away from Evercreech Junction with the 4.20pm Templecombe-Bath on 17 July 1965. The goods shed and sidings behind the down platform still seem to be reasonably well used. Photograph Hugh Ballantyne.

2P 4-4-0 No.40652 pilots 5MT 4-6-0 No.73047 on a Bournemouth-bound train on 4 July 1959. The train is approaching Evercreech Junction from Bath, the junction with the Highbridge branch (the one-time Somerset Central main line) being clearly discernible. Photograph R.E. Toop.

passengers are required at all the stations where there are loop lines...'`, but , on the whole, things were not that simple. Indeed, Col. Rich later conceded in private that *'...never had such a line, with such heavy works on it, been* *presented in the state in which the Bath extension was when I first went over it'.*

Nevertheless, the line opened on 20 July, but as if to set an unfortunate precedent the first public train from Bath was so late that it missed the connection with the LSWR train at Templecombe. Punctuality - or, rather, a lack of it - wasn't the S&D's only problem. As explained later by the Board of Trade inspector, Col. Yolland: *'...considerable portions of the line were*

EVERCREECH JUNCTION

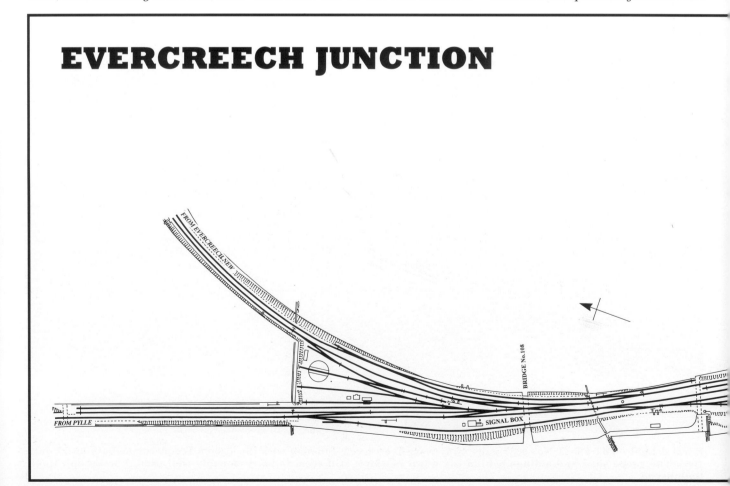

A local to Templecombe, hauled by 3F 0-6-0 No.43218, approaches Evercreech Junction on 1 June 1957. The engine had been built in 1902 to a standard Derby design for the S&D Joint, and until 1930 wore S&DJ No.72. Photograph R.E. Toop.

constructed during very dry weather and the material of which some of the embankments were formed (the lias clay) is such as to make it very difficult to keep them up after much rain .....and there has been a considerable quantity of rain since this Branch Line was opened ...and there have been many subsidences and slips'. The dubious condition of the line was invariably given as the reason for the irregularity of the trains, which initially comprised thirteen down and eleven up each day. One point of interest - in the above extract Col. Yolland referred to the extension as the 'branch line' although the moment the line had opened it had been regarded as the main line, the older line between Evercreech and Burnham having assumed the status of branch. The new main line was regarded as 'down' in a southbound direction but the branch was 'up' from Evercreech Junction to Burnham - i.e. a journey on

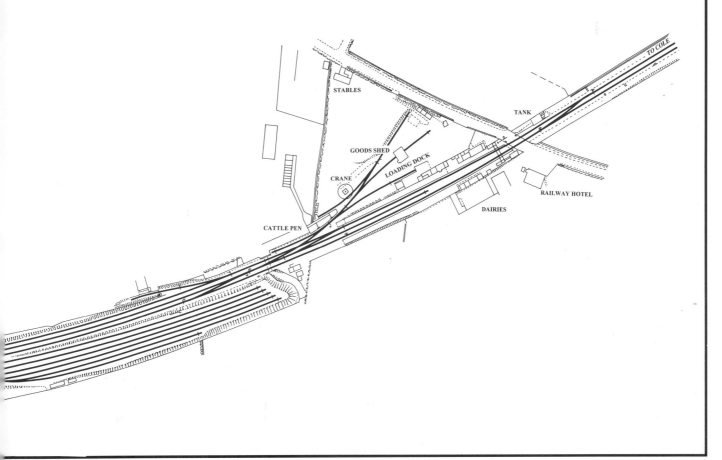

An up passenger train - possibly a Templecombe-Bath local - arrives, with 4F 0-6-0 No.44523 in charge. In the middle road, Ivatt 2-6-2T No.41304 waits with what, presumably, is a Highbridge branch train; this train will move to the platform road after the Bath train has cleared the section. The date is 1 June 1957. Photograph R.E. Toop.

the 'old' main line from Bournemouth to Burnham would be 'up' throughout, but a trip from Bath to Burnham required a nominal change of direction at Evercreech Junction.

The condition of the Bath extension caused a major problem on Monday 5 October 1874. On that day, the 6.20am Templecombe - Bath passenger train - the first northbound train of the day - reached Evercreech Junction at 7.03am and left one minute later. The train consisted of engine and tender (2-4-0 No.18 - built by George England in 1865 and with-

On 1 June 1957, 4F 0-6-0 No.44559 (one-time S&DJ No.59) waits with a down train, while Ivatt 2-6-2T No.41304 arrives with what is probably a Templecombe-Bath local. The distinctive water tower can be seen on the other side of the level crossing - it supplied the water column between the platforms. Another distinctive piece of local hardware was the extremely tall down starting signal. Photograph R.E. Toop.

The Standard 5MTs arrived on the S&D in 1954, and subsequently had a respectable innings on the line. Here, No.75073 takes on water before resuming its journey from Bath to Bournemouth on 1 June 1957. In the distance - beyond the level crossing - one can see how the line rose on its way towards Cole. Photograph R.E. Toop.

drawn in 1897 - which had recently been given 'heavy boiler and general repairs' and was considered to be in good condition), a brake van, one second class carriage, one third class and one first class (in that order). The train was travelling at about 15mph when, at the start of the gentle left-hand curve on the approach to Pecking Mill Viaduct, the engine '...gradually diverged from the right rail until it came into contact with the right parapet wall of the Viaduct, broke it down, and fell over the eastern side of the viaduct, which is about 22 feet in height at that part, and it was followed by the tender and the guard's break van...' The engine driver, George Carter (a 'very good

The 4.19pm milk and perishables van from Highbridge has been brought into Evercreech Junction by 3F No.43436. The date is 1 June 1957. Photograph R.E. Toop.

Three expectant pilot engines wait on the centre road at Evercreech Junction on 4 July 1959. It's a bit difficult to tell, but they look like a pair of 4-4-0s and an 0-6-0. This view looks in the up direction - i.e. to the north-west. The centre road was not always a dead-end - it once extended past the southern end of the station, and shunting manoeuvres at that end usually resulted in the level crossing being closed to road traffic for what was considered, in some quarters, an unacceptable length of time. Photograph R.E. Toop.

driver and a very steady man') was fatally injured, the fireman and guard sustaining serious but survivable injuries, and the inspector being 'slightly bruised'. Although the passenger carriages were all derailed they remained upright and did not fall over the viaduct, and the passengers all escaped unhurt.

The obligatory Board of Trade enquiry into the accident was headed by Col. Yolland who noted that on the approach to the scene of the accident - i.e. where the derailment had actually occurred - the left-hand rail had sunk approximately eight inches and the right-hand rail by some three inches. Subsidence had indeed played

34043

3F 0-6-0 No.43216 (ex-SDJR No.72) approaches Evercreech Junction North with the 4.0pm ex-Highbridge, 22 July 1958. Photograph R.C. Riley.

havoc, but the chief ganger opined that, although the rails had had to be lifted at that very spot (due to settlement of the embankment) three times in late September and early October, the ground had seemed to be satisfactory on the day before the accident. There were recriminations regarding the procedure for inspecting the line each morning prior to the passage of the first train of the day, but Col. Yolland had a few perceptive words to say about the manner in which the line had been built. He was not slow to refer to Col. Rich's earlier comments about the way the line had first been presented for inspection, and he pointedly remarked that it was unusual for the contractor (who had built the line) to have passed all responsibility to the railway company at the moment the line had been opened to traffic - normally, contractors retained responsibility for their works for one

Stirring stuff on 6 July 1959 - 34043 COMBE MARTIN on the down Pines passes 34044 WOOLACOMBE with empty stock. Adjacent numbers and both of them *combes!* Photograph R.C. Riley.

An up train waits at Evercreech Junction, 22 July 1958 - the middle road holds stock rather that the familiar line of pilots. This view was taken from the footbridge which crossed the line at the southern end of the station. Photograph R.C. Riley.

year after a line had opened. The S&D's arrangement had, however, been dictated by its difficulty in footing the contractors' bills.

The Bath extension - and its less than perfect ride - did not escape the attentions of the irascible Ernest Ahrons, who wrote about his journeys on the line in the late 1870s: *'The old dark green engines were not much to look at, as far as appearance and somewhat diminutive size went, but when it came to running down banks of 1 in 50 at high speeds they were very much all there. As they could do little more than crawl up one side of the bank, the drivers made amends by letting the engines out for all they were worth down the other side.*

Further, since the trains consisted of four-wheeled coaches, the age of which was extremely uncertain, the side-to-side motion was somewhat appalling, especially between Binegar and Evercreech Junction, where I more than once thought that my days were about to end'.

Near the end..... 19 February 1966. This general view looks north from Evercreech Junction, the main line to Bath veering off right and the branch to Highbridge heading slightly to the right of the North signalbox. Photograph Hugh Ballantyne.

As far back as the 1870s, the level crossing with the main road (now the A361) at the south-east end of Evercreech Junction was a real trouble spot for road users. The pub on the left still stands - it's now called the Natterjack, or something similar. Photograph H.C. Casserley.

Crossing the Line

Returning to 1874, Col. Yolland was back at Evercreech Junction on 20 November to adjudicate on alleged delays to road traffic using the level crossing at the southern end of the station, the Trustees of the Shepton Mallet turnpike having cited delays of 'twenty minutes or half an hour'. The Trustees hardly got off to a flying start with Col. Yolland, his report noting that:

'I was met by the Secretary and Engineer of the Somerset & Dorset Company, but no one appeared on behalf of the Trustees, although I wasted some time beyond the hour that I had named.

'In addition to the two lines of railway at this station which were laid down when I reported on January 29th 1874, there is now a third line, used as a spare line intermediate between the Up and Down main lines, so constructed that nothing can be brought out of this spare line at the south-eastern end of the Station, and then placed either on the Up or Down main lines without being shunted across the turnpike road'.

The S&D explained that shunting manoeuvres across the road were no longer undertaken, and so Col. Yolland put the ball in the Trustees' court by inviting them to prove their allegations regarding delays to traffic. Stalemate, as usual, ensued. Nevertheless, the layout at the south-eastern end of the station was radically altered at a later date; access to the middle line (the 'spare intermediate line') was severed at that end, with access subsequently being from the north-west end only. Unfortunately, it has proved impossible to determine when that change was made, although the new layout was clearly operational by (or probably long before) 1 October 1911, when Major Pringle reported for the Board of Trade on the subject of... delays to vehicular traffic at the level crossing:

'The public road (Shepton Mallet to Castle Cary) is crossed by two lines of rail, the up and down respectively, and the crossing immediately adjoins the south

No.34042 DORCHESTER with the down Pines Express, at Evercreech Junction, 14 April 1962. The Mogul, class 4 No.75023, had piloted the Pacific over the Mendips and while 34042 took water, had uncoupled and drawn forward, to then set back on to the up line, leaving the road clear for the express to continue southwards. Photograph Ivo Peters.

The 1.10pm down stopper, Bath to Bournemouth West behind EVENING STAR on 12 September 1962. Photograph Ivo Peters.

Bath 2-8-0 No.48468 on a three coach train, the 1.10pm down local from Bath, 21 September 1963. Photograph Ivo Peters.

The assisting engines (all are 2P 4-4-0s) lined up in the middle road on a summer Saturday morning, 12 August 1958. Such a situation was unusual, in that generally one or two 4F 0-6-0s would be part of the cavalcade. The 2Ps are 40563, 40568, 40700, 40564 and 40697. Photograph Ivo Peters.

end of the station platforms. Double gates are fitted to the crossing which fence in both roadway and railway respectively. These gates, which are normally open for vehicular traffic along the public road, are closed and opened by the signalman in Evercreech Junction South signal box, by means of a gatewheel, and are interlocked with the up and down line signals. There is an excellent view of the level crossing and its approaches from the signal box which is placed at the south end of the up platform. There is a footbridge available for foot passengers.

'The general arrangements negate the idea of danger arising at the level crossing, and the Rural District Council, I understand concur in this view. The Council's complaint has reference to the frequent and lengthy delays which are experienced by the vehicular traffic...

''I pointed out to the representatives of the Rural District Council that as danger could not be diagnosed, the Board [of Trade] had no power to require the construction of a bridge over or under the railway. Also, as the crossing was authorised by a special Act of 1856 prior to the Railway Clauses Act, 1863, it would not be possible to apply the provisions of the latter regarding the prohibition of shunting on level crossings.

'So far as the total number of vehicles stopped is concerned, the returns show that during the hours of daylight the proportion is not greater that 10 per cent. But there appear to be sometimes delays extending to about 7 minutes, which are

due to shunting movements etc., and it is to these lengthy periods that strong exception is taken. [A census of road traffic had been taken on 16 and 17 May 1911, and showed that 16 and 29 vehicles had been delayed out of 271 and 302 respectively; furthermore, no delay on those two days had exceeded three minutes].

'With reference to these movements I wish to draw the attention of the Railway Company to the following:

(a) The watering of goods or empty stock trains at the up [northbound] starting signal (in its present position) should be entirely prohibited, when such trains are long enough to foul the level crossing.

(b) The gates in the case of shunting passenger or other vehicles from one plat-

2P 4-4-0 No.40564 and Black 5 4-6-0 No.45440 with the up Pines Express charge off from Evercreech Junction for the start of the climb to Masbury Summit, 12 August 1950. On the middle road is Johnson 0-4-4T No.58047 with a down local for Templecombe. Photograph Ivo Peters.

Black 5 No.44839 in Evercreech Junction with the down Pines amid driving wind and rain, 8 April 1950. Whilst the 4-6-0 takes water the assisting 2P, No.40634, drew forward and set back on to the up road, to get out of 44839's way before it resumed its journey down to Bournemouth. Photograph Ivo Peters.

form road to the other via the south end crossover should be, whenever road vehicles are waiting to use the level crossing, opened during the shunting operation, after the railway vehicles have passed from one side to the other.

(c) Goods trains whenever it is found necessary to shunt them from one running road to another should be handled at Evercreech North Junction whenever possible'.

The eventual solution to the seemingly perpetual problem? The Appendix to the service timetable (this extract is from the 1933 edition) explains: **'Public level crossing:** *No engine or train or portion of a train shall be permitted to stand on or to shunt over the level crossing of the turnpike road so as to prevent the gates from being closed across the railway, and no persons travelling along the road shall be detained for a longer interval of time than 5 minutes by the gates remaining closed against them'.*

Everyday Life

Most of the line between Templecombe and Bath was eventually doubled, albeit in a piecemeal manner, the ten and a half miles southwards from Evercreech Junction

New BR 4MTs Nos.75072 and 75073, leaving Evercreech Junction with the 2.45pm SO Bournemouth to Bristol, 30 June 1956. Photograph Ivo Peters.

4F 0-6-0 No.44135 entering Evercreech Junction, 6 July 1959, with the 3.40pm Bournemouth West-Bristol. Photograph R.C. Riley.

to Templecombe being doubled in 1884 and the two and a quarter mile section northwards to Evercreech in August 1886. The obligatory Board of Trade report noted that the second line of rails was '...of the new standard pattern adopted on the Midland Railway...'.

Evercreech Junction settled down to a relatively routine existence, warranting little attention, it would seem, from the Joint Committee. Among the few mentions in the minute books is an item dated 3 August 1904: '...the engineer reported that the actual cost of carrying out the renewal of the turntable at Evercreech Junction will be about £2,047, or £283 in excess of the first estimate'`. The infrequency of the station's appearances in the minute books was *not*, however, a reflection of its trade, the goods traffic, in particular, being far from insignificant - circa 1910 some 900 wagons were attached or detached at Evercreech Junction daily. As well as the marshalling of wagons, general goods were dealt with at the goods shed behind the down platform, and there were also sidings serving a slaughterhouse and a brick and tile works.   Around 1910 new works were undertaken at the station, with the obligatory BoT inspection executed by Major Pringle in March 1911. The report itself was standard fare, but it gave an insight into part of the contemporary signalling arrangements:

'A new trailing connection has been laid with the up branch line which provides access to a siding or shunting neck on the west side of the railway lines. A new

ground signal has been provided for controlling the movement of traffic out of the siding.

'The new connection is worked from Evercreech North Junction Signal Box, which contains an old frame with 32 levers, all in use; four of these are "push and pull" levers.

'There is an advanced signal on the single lines towards Highbridge to limit the extent of or to protect shunting movements, but the blocking back signal must in accordance with instructions be sent to the next block post during such time as the branch is open for traffic, and acknowledged before the single line is occupied by shunting operations'.

The S&D line as a whole came under the scrutiny of the Joint Committee in 1922, when yet another economy drive was being planned. Specific recommendations were made regarding possible savings at Evercreech Junction:

'There are five sets of Drivers and Firemen and two water pumping enginemen stationed at this Junction for relieving purposes under the supervision of the District Locomotive Superintendent at Bath. These Drivers and Firemen should all be considered in connection with the remodelling of the Bath roster; therefore, the Commission do not make any further recommendation in reference to them.

''In view of the extension of the marshalling sidings at Evercreech Junction, a work now in progress with the object, it is understood, of closing the Lower Yard at Templecombe; also having regard to the convenient position from a working point of view this station [Evercreech

Junction] occupies on the Joint Line, the Commission gave careful consideration to a suggestion that an up-to-date Locomotive Running Shed should be constructed there, which, coupled with a remodelled Goods train service might, it was thought, result in such a saving in running expenses as would justify the expenditure the proposal would entail.

'It was ascertained, however, that a large proportion of the goods traffic passing over the Joint Line consists of through traffic from the Midland to the South Western system, necessitating the running of full train loads from Bath to Templecombe which do not, of course, require to be broken up en route, so that locomotive sheds of practically the present capacity would still have to be retained at Templecombe.

'In these circumstances, also bearing in mind the uncertain future of the Joint Line on its operating side, the Commission are of the opinion that they cannot, at this juncture, recommend a heavy capital expenditure which the erection of a shed and the provision of housing accommodation for the staff would involve'.

At the grouping, the S&D came under the joint control of the LMSR and the Southern, but a revision of arrangements in January 1930 resulted in the LMSR assuming full responsibility for motive power and taking into stock the S&D locomotives, which had hitherto had their own numbering system and livery.

Locomotives
Until 1891, when the S&D acquired the first of its Derby-built 4-4-0s, the

Standard Class 5 4-6-0 No.73028 shunting an up freight, 6 July 1959. Photograph R.C. Riley.

main line passenger services were handled almost exclusively by 2-4-0s - not the most suitable of engines, given the ferocious gradients north of Evercreech. Branch and local passenger workings were customarily worked by 2-4-0Ts or 0-4-4Ts, the latter type - again, virtually a standard Midland design - making its debut in 1877. For many years the goods duties fell, inevitably, to 0-6-0s, some of which had their origins in 'independent' days and others (with an unmistakable Midland pedigree) in Joint Committee days, but in 1914 the first of the S&D's celebrated '7F' 2-8-0s appeared (see *BRILL* 4:9). The 2-8-0s were used principally on the Bath - Templecombe section, and performed their fair share of workings to and from the goods yard at Evercreech Junction.

There was another important addition to the roll-call of S&D locomotives. When the Bath extension opened in 1874, the S&D was very mindful of the need for banking engines on the steeply graded line - not only to assist trains up the hills, but also to provide extra braking power *down* the hills. For such duties nine sturdy 0-6-0STs were purchased from Fox Walker (although the last two weren't delivered until 'joint' days), and eight of those nine engines survived until the 1930s. At Evercreech Junction, the banking (and pilot) engines waited on the dead-end siding which had been laid between the platform roads, the generous space between the platforms being a legacy of the original intention to lay mixed

gauge rails between Glastonbury and Cole.

As train weights increased - especially when Midland bogie corridor stock started to appear on through workings - the need for banking/

piloting on the weekend and summer season trains became more intense. Between Evercreech Junction and Bath, the maximum load permitted for an unassisted engine was 200 tons (270 tons for the 'Black Fives', which

Pannier tank 4631 sets off with the 2.20pm local from Highbridge to Templecombe, on 12 June 1965. Photograph Ivo Peters.

first appeared on the S&D in 1938) but while such loading limits were often adequate for off-season weekday trains, it could be a very different matter on summer Saturdays. Over the years, most of the engine types used on the S&D were employed, albeit with varying regularity, on banking or pilot duties over the Mendips. On a typical summer Saturday, however, there was usually a problem with the direction and the timing of the rush-

additional track occupation.

By the early 1950s (if not before), a solution of sorts had been found to the unevenness of banking and piloting requirements on summer Saturday peaks. As already explained, in the morning the majority of assistance was required by northbound trains, but Templecombe shed (ten miles to the south of Evercreech Junction) could not be expected to fill *all* the requirements and so additional en-

By the mid-1950s Evercreech Junction had become used to the sight of 'Black Fives', lightweight Bulleid Pacifics and Standard 5MT 4-6-0s on the through trains. The first Pacific to work the line is believed to have been No.21C149 (as it then was) which on 6 November 1948 had hauled a football special from Bournemouth to Bristol, although the regular use of 4-6-2s on the S&D didn't commence until 1951. The main line goods work-

Class 4 Mogul No.76027 on the 12.55pm up from Bournemouth pulls away from Evercreech Junction in fine fashion, 12 March 1955. Photograph Ivo Peters.

the bulk of the northbound traffic (i.e. trains carrying holidaymakers *returning from* the South Coast) traversed the line in the morning, while the heaviest traffic heading southward *to the* coast traversed the line in the afternoon. Consequently, it was impossible to balance the majority of the assisting duties by having, say, a northbound pilot turn round at Bath and return as pilot to the next southbound train. The option of sending a pilot back to its starting point light engine was a non-starter, partly on the grounds of economy and partly due to

gines had to be supplied by Bath. Mainly to reduce the track occupation, the Bath engines (usually 4-4-0s) were dispatched to Evercreech Junction piloting comparatively lightly-loaded trains such as the 8.15am and 9.55am locals from Bath. In the northbound direction most pilot engines that were attached at Evercreech Junction worked through to Bath, but at the busiest times some of the assisting engines were detached at Binegar (having negotiated Masbury Summit) and then ran back tender-first to Evercreech Junction.

ings at that time were usually handled by the 7F 2-8-0s or 0-6-0s, although the 2-8-0s didn't often venture south of Templecombe (again, see *BRILL* 4:9). The other line at Evercreech Junction - the branch to Highbridge and Burnham - was worked for many years principally by 0-4-4Ts or 0-6-0s, the latter including ex-S&D 'Bulldogs' which had started their lives in the mid-1890s on freight duties on the Bath extension. From the mid-1950s ex-LMSR Ivatt 2-6-2Ts were introduced on the branch, and remained until the cessation of passenger serv-

2-8-0 No.53808 with the 10.40am SO Exmouth to Cleethorpes on 2 July 1960; 3F 0-6-0 No.43734 stands on the middle road with the 1.20pm local for Highbridge. Photograph Ivo Peters.

48309 arriving with the 1.10pm down local. Photograph Ivo Peters.

Passenger workings at Evercreech Junction, taken from the summer 1952 public timetable (departure times from Evercreech Junction unless otherwise stated):

N.B: In all cases, trains ran to/from Bournemouth West, not Bournemouth Central.

SO *	4.00am #	Sheffield-Bournemouth
SO *	4.15am #	Derby-Bournemouth
SO	4.45am #	Bradford-Bournemouth
SO	9.55am #	Bristol TM-Bournemouth
SO	11.30am #	Birmingham-Bournemouth
	7.24am	Templecombe-Bath
Arr.	8.00am	ex-Highbridge
	8.15am	Bristol TM-Bournemouth
	8.20am	to Highbridge
Arr.	9.00am	ex-Templecombe
SO *	9.25am	Bournemouth-Sheffield (express)
	9.38am	Templecombe-Bath
	9.40am	Bath-Templecombe
	9.55am	to Highbridge
SO	10.20am	Bournemouth-Bradford
SX	10.48am	ex-Bournemouth
SX	10.50am	Evercreech Junct-Wincanton
SO	10.50am	Bournemouth-Liverpool
Arr.	10.53am	ex-Highbridge
	11.02am	Bournemouth-Manchester ('Pines Express')
	11.07am	Bristol TM-Bournemouth
MFO	11.18am	Bournemouth-Sheffield (express)
SO	11.20am	Bournemouth-Sheffield (express)
SO	11.48am	Bournemouth-Cleethorpes (express)
SO	12.03pm	Bournemouth-Manchester (express)
	12.24pm	Templecombe-Bath
SO *	12.40pm	Bournemouth-Derby (express)
SO	1.02pm	Nottingham-Bournemouth (express)
SX	1.03pm	Bournemouth-Gloucester (express)
SO	1.10pm	Bournemouth-Sheffield (express)
SX	1.15pm	to Highbridge
SO	1.20pm	to Highbridge
SO	2.28pm	Bath-Templecombe
SX	2.28pm	Bath-Bailey Gate
	3.02pm	Bournemouth-Bristol St.Philip's
SO	3.12pm	Cleethorpes-Bournemouth
	3.23pm	Highbridge-Templecombe
SO *	3.35pm	Sheffield-Bournemouth (express)
MFO	3.45pm	Sheffield-Bournemouth (express)
SO	3.53pm	Bradford- Bournemouth (express)
SX	4.00pm	Manchester-Bournemouth ('Pines Express')
SO	4.10pm	Evercreech Junct-Templecombe
SX	4.10pm	Evercreech Junct-Bournemouth
SO *	4.20pm	Bournemouth West-Bristol TM (express)
SX	4.36pm	Bath-Templecombe
SO	4.38pm	Manchester-Bournemouth ('Pines Express')
	4.42pm	Templecombe-Bath
	4.48pm	to Highbridge
Arr.	5.18pm	ex-Highbridge
SO *	5.23pm	Liverpool-Bournemouth (express)
SX	5.27pm	Gloucester-Bournemouth
SO	5.36pm	Manchester-Bournemouth (express)
	5.55pm	Bournemouth-Bristol St.Philip's
SX	5.56pm	Bath-Bournemouth
	6.00pm	to Highbridge
Arr.	8.10pm	ex-Highbridge
	8.25pm	Bristol St.Philip's-Bournemouth
SO	8.50pm	Bournemouth-Bristol TM
	9.17pm	Templecombe-Bath
	9.25pm	to Highbridge

* Train did not run for whole period of timetable
# Estimated passing time of non-stop train.

Sundays: There was only one advertised working on the S&D on Sundays during the summer of 1952. It was a Bristol - Bournemouth West return working - the down train did not call at Evercreech Junction, but the up train did (dep. 8.33pm).

anon - there were changes in the types of motive power on the Highbridge branch, ex-GWR 2251 0-6-0s and 57XX 0-6-0PTs being used in conjunction with LMR 0-6-0s and Ivatt 2-6-2Ts. The WR take-over had little outward effect on the motive power situation on the main line, the only significant changes coming in 1960 when Standard 9F 2-10-0s were drafted to the S&D and in 1963 when ex-LMSR 8F 2-8-0s moved in - clearly, though, neither the 9Fs nor 8Fs were standard GWR products, despite the construction of several of both types at Swindon - and so Evercreech Junction continued to see the customary mix - mainly 4-4-0s, 4-6-0s, 0-6-0s and 7F 2-8-0s.

Services

The summer season brought a fair old variety of long-distance through workings to the S&D line, all of the up trains and most of the down ones - alleged 'expresses' included - usually calling at Evercreech Junction. In the early 1950s the summer Saturday public timetables usually showed around ten or so expresses in each direction plus two or three Bristol - Bournemouth trains. The traditional 'holiday weeks' - usually in mid-August - in some Midlands and North Country industrial towns brought an additional quota of reliefs and specials. The best-known of all the trains on the S&D line was, of course, the 'Pines Express' although, as with some other workings on the line, the word 'express' must be used in a rather loose context in connection with the S&D. As for the 'Pines', it had started life as an un-named Manchester - Bournemouth express in 1910, had been discontinued in 1914, but had been reinstated and in 1927 it assumed its familiar title.

On the Evercreech Junction - Highbridge branch, the services during the 1950s usually comprised six up (i.e. westbound) trains and five down on weekdays, one or two of the down trains working through to Templecombe. The branch workings were 'all stations' affairs - a far cry from the 1890s when a fast Templecombe - Bridgwater train, connecting with a LSWR express at Templecombe, had been advertised to pass through Evercreech Junction non-stop. It has often been remarked that the lack of a branch bay at Evercreech Junction added to the occasional melee on summer Saturdays, but it must be remembered that the peak season at Evercreech Junction comprised something like ten days out of the whole year and hardly justified the cost of remedial action.

As mentioned earlier, the goods traffic on the main line to and through Evercreech Junction was far from insignificant, the through trains usually being to or from Templecombe where traffic was exchanged with the SR. The goods yard at Evercreech saw steady

ices. The scheduled passenger services on the branch were, incidentally, truncated at Highbridge as from 29 October 1951, although excursion trains continued to work right through to Burnham until September 1962.

As a result of boundary changes on 1 February 1958, the whole of the S&D north of Henstridge passed lock, stock and barrel to the Western Region. Apart from major changes to the line's administration - more of which

48309 again. Photograph Ivo Peters.

action through the day and for much of the night, the appendix to the WTT (for 1933, in this instance) stipulating that:

'Evercreech Junction - engines whistling: Under no circumstances must a shunter or other person engaged in shunting operations at the station or junction instruct a driver to give engine whistles to intimate the up or down line is clear, but the bell signals as prescribed must in each case be properly signalled on the bell instrument by the shunter in charge to the signalman on duty in the respective boxes.

'Extra vehicles for detaching: Guards of passenger trains must arrange to wire Evercreech Junction when they have extra vehicles on their trains to be detached there, stating the position of such vehicles on the trains'.

After the Western Region took over the S&D in 1958, it appeared to many that there was a policy of deliberately running down the entire line. Admittedly, the S&D had a lot against it - it was a penetrating line, it was a cross-country route, and for much of its length it wasn't particularly easy to work, but even the most hardened re-

alist couldn't deny that the WR's attitude to it was more than a little questionable. A hefty nail in the S&D's rapidly closing coffin came on 10 September 1962 when all through trains were withdrawn. These included the 'Pines Express', which was subsequently re-routed via Oxford, Reading and Basingstoke, and summer Saturday Cleethorpes - Exmouth/Sidmouth trains, which had been operated during the 1960, 1961 and 1962 seasons. The local trains lingered on until the closure of the line in 1966, the originally scheduled closure date of 3 Janu-

Ivatt tank with the rather extravagant tall version of the chimney comes past Evercreech Junction North with the 5.0pm to Highbridge, 22 July 1958. Photograph R.C. Riley.

Pacific 34044 WOOLACOMBE on an up ECS passes 5MT No.73028, 6 July 1959. Photograph R.C.Riley.

ary having to be postponed when one of the road transport operators pulled out. The S&D - the main line and the Highbridge branch - finally closed on 7 March 1966.

Afterwards.....

Today, the disused station at Evercreech Junction is still clearly discernible on the west side of the A371

Shepton Mallet - Castle Cary road. After the station closed, it was acquired for conversion into a private house - it remains as such today and, therefore, is *not* accessible to the public. On the east side of the road, the trackbed of the railway (in the direction of Templecombe) can be easily seen, but it is desperately overgrown and offers no real scope for walking.

The pub alongside the station - once called the Railway Inn - was renamed, after the closure of the station, as the 'Silent Whistle', but it has had at least one other change of identity since then.

Thanks are due to Eric Youldon for his invaluable assistance with this article.

2-8-0 53809 shunting a freight (ex-Bath) on 6 July 1959. Photograph R.C.Riley.

FOURUM
When Coal Was King

Above: To most 'main line' enthusiasts, the world of industrial locomotives was one of life's great mysteries - if it wasn't in the fabled *Combined Volume*, it hardly had a claim to proper existence. Putting things into perspective, that was a little odd, for depending on regional upbringing, most enthusiasts could tell you *something* about the locomotives of, say, the Plymouth, Devonport & South Western Junction Railway, the Rhondda & Swansea Bay, the Hull & Barnsley, or the Furness, but there was one particular industrial user who had more locomotives that those four 'main line' examples combined. That industrial giant was the National Coal Board. When taking stock of NCB railway activities, it wasn't just a succession of industrial pugs, as some have dismissed this varied and rewarding field of study. The locomotives, the operations - the whole gamut of railway activities, in fact - were sometimes on a more expansive scale than could be seen at many 'main line' locations. This preamble serves however, a covert purpose too - as suitable herald for *RAILWAY BYLINES* magazine, the new Irwell Press alternate (and alternative!) monthly publication dealing with minor and industrial railways - NCB included. Buy a copy and just *feel* the coal dust......

This splendid picture, by the way, shows Sunderland Staiths on the River Wear. The locomotive is NCB No.17, a Manning Wardle 0-4-0ST (W/No.2023) of 1923 vintage, pulling a train of empties away from the hoist on 3 May 1955. Photograph Neville Stead Collection.

Below: The Mid-East Durham (No.2) Area of the NCB took in, roughly speaking, the land to the south of Sunderland and the River Wear. This included Philadelphia Colliery, from where green liveried NCB 0-6-2T No.57 (built by Hawthorn Leslie in 1934) started its journey with a trainload of coal for Lambton Staiths. The train is passing through Pallion station (on the Sunderland-Penshaw line); the year is 1963. Photograph Ian S. Carr.

Above: NCB Mid-East Durham Area once again - this time the location is the old Lambton, Hetton & Joicey workshops at Philadelphia Colliery and the date is June 1961. The locomotive in the foreground, NCB 0-6-0PT No.6, had an interesting pedigree in that it was constructed at the Philadelphia Works in 1958, partly from components salvaged from two ancient Coulthard 0-6-0s, which dated back to 1864. Photograph Phil Lynch.

Below: To some, the mention of industrial railways conjures up images of unkempt locomotives with liveries hardly discernible through layers of grime, and ramshackle buildings which would have horrified any self-respecting structural inspector. That might have held true in some cases, but dare one suggest that this scene displays a somewhat better standard of maintenance than might be found at certain main line locations. Sunlight penetrates the inner sanctum of the engine shed at Philadelphia Colliery. Simmering inside are NCB No.31, a Kitson 0-6-2T (W/No.4533 of 1907) and No.57, a Hawthorn Leslie 0-6-2T, (W/No.3834 of 1934). Don't forget - there's more of this in every issue of *RAILWAY BYLINES*, every other month. Photograph Phil Lynch.

A STRANGE TRANSFORMATION

There could be no more eloquent testimony to Kirkby shed's role in life - to move coal. The shed was put there to secure the Midland's share in the burgeoning trade, and the enormous spoil heap bears witness to the rightness of this policy. The row of hybrid huts opposite the turntable was the local control. 1st January 1959.

By Ian Sixsmith

As the 1950s drew to a close, though the *notion* of dieselisation and electrification had penetrated most corners of the network, in 1957 the *reality* seemed still far off. The shattered pieces of a rolling programme of improvements at engine sheds had been taken up with an increasing vigour after the War, and in truth there were many gaps to fill. The East Midlands was profitable for coal - good quality stuff in a booming area which represented a captive traffic for BR. Kirkby

in Ashfield lay at the heart of this and existed really, to move coal and little else. An indication of the value of the traffic was the sending, new, of 8F 2-8-0s in the 1930s, to give a fleet of nearly forty. The old Midland three road shed was overcrowded and ageing; it had opened in 1903 and housed under cover nine or twelve locos (depending on the size taken as 'standard'). The 1945 allocation numbered nearly seventy locos!

The BR rebuilding programme lumbered into action (almost for the

last time) in 1958, when the contractors turned up at Kirkby; it was misleading to relate allocation to the amount of cover available (it always had been so) but at Kirkby matters had slipped a bit far. So it was that a new two road extension was ordered. Now this was hardly generous but was doubtless greatly appreciated by the staff - the old three road shed for instance, did not even have pits *outside* - not only a stupidly onerous imposition but a thoroughly dangerous one too. The real heart of the modernisa-

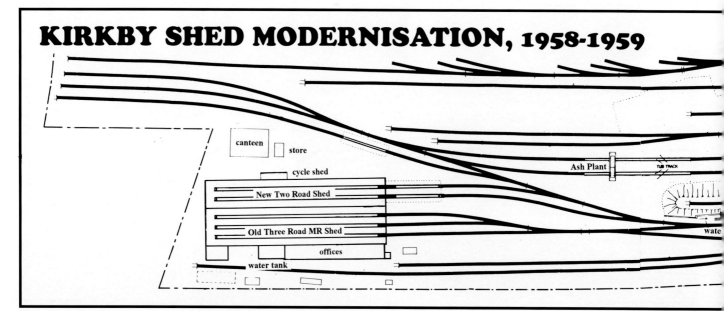

KIRKBY SHED MODERNISATION, 1958-1959

canteen store

cycle shed

New Two Road Shed

Old Three Road MR Shed

offices

water tank

Ash Plant TUB TRACK

wate

Another steam and smoke-wreathed view from the new coaler, 1st October 1958. A further odd thing about Kirkby's modernisation was that it was not *comprehensive,* at least in the sense of the LMS works of the 1930s. The whole idea then had been to decrease the time out of traffic and in turn decrease the number of locomotives needed. The ideal was the 'cafeteria' system which meant locos proceeded smoothly and without interruption through the full sequence of coaling, ash disposal and turning. At Kirkby, modernisation stopped short of the turning component - and the turntable remained out on its ancient Midland Railway limb. It was no great disadvantage, for Kirkby was a medium size shed after all. Yet study the plan; at peak times engines could only back up and wait while the one in front reversed off the 'table. A 'dead end' which was anathema to the planners of the 1930s.

tion at Kirkby, however, was not the new covered accommodation available but, *at last,* mechanised coal and ash disposal was finally an option. In this way, the constant procession of 8Fs would be turned round with far greater facility - the investment however was far from inconsiderable, and the returns were calculated on a similar basis to locomotives - 25 to 30 years-worth of work were expected from the new plant. In 1957-1958 of course, this

was more or less conceivable; although steam was expected to last 'to the 1970s' there was a camp which (sensibly, with hindsight) foresaw certain areas and certain traffics as being ideal for lingering outposts of steam. Were not considerable numbers of 9Fs, as well as other locos, still on order? Kirkby would be an ideal 'outpost' - the area was unlikely to attract electrification until late, if at all, the country would always need coal (wouldn't

it?), there was a 'mono-traffic' (a feature which had brought the large numbers of 8Fs in the first place), nearly-new locos would be available (surely no railway would scrap a fleet of steam locos ten or so years old - they wouldn't be allowed to - would they?) and - the clincher - the fuel for these locos lay all about, and even *underneath* them - it couldn't be cheaper. Could it?

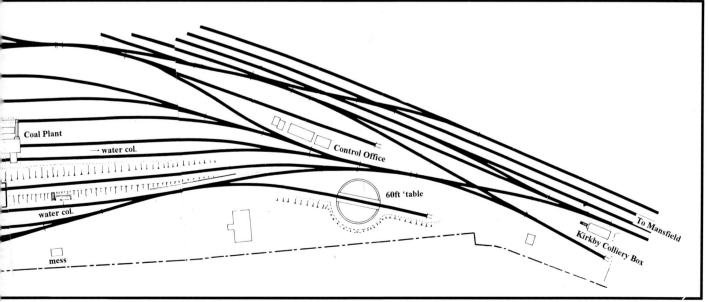

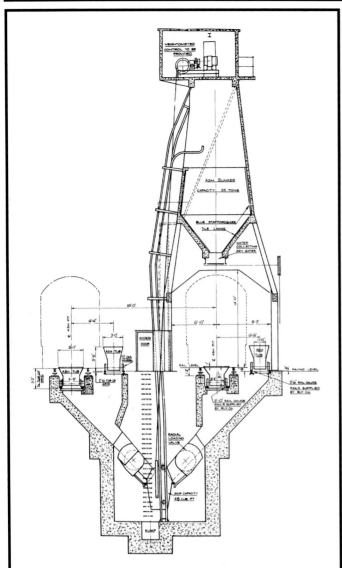

Here and right: Final form of British ash tower, of the type put up at Kirkby in Ashfield.

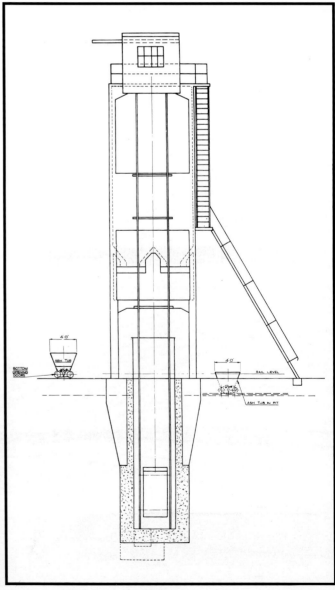

Left: The new Kirkby coal and ash towers, 1st January 1959. Behind lays the old Midland manual coal stage; it would once have had a pitched roof, but newish brickwork indicates that it has been 'smoothed off'. Retained, the stage would afterwards provide a useful 'spare', for, whatever their advantages, mechanical coalers inevitably needed some maintenance, whilst some individual examples had a less than perfect record of reliability.

Far left: The ash tower with coaler beyond, 1st January 1959. The new water cranes put in look to be of the 'semi-automatic' type whereby the flow was started by drawing the jib downwards - hence the very short 'bag'.

Below: A comparison in styling, 1st January 1959. The new shed at least had pits outside, a feature which the Midland, despite all its attention to detail, seems to have ignored. An omission all the more surprising in that all its big contemporaries - GW, LNW and so on - seem to have regarded such pits as *de rigueur*.

Left: In one obvious respect, the new building was marked apart from its predecessor alongside, and that was in the lack of any concession whatsoever to style or proportion of line in the design itself. Without doubt, it was, especially in so close a conjunction with the turn of the century elegance of the MR shed - ugly. Various pipes and so on are left over from the new work on 5th November 1958, and someone seems to have over-ordered a section of the asbestos smoke chuting. Thinking on't, it is more likely to be a damaged piece, broken in transit (despite being tied up in straw in an open wagon) or dropped during installation.

Below: Kirkby with resident (specially balanced for extra speed - hence the star under the number) on 5th November 1958. This, if you like, was the final form of straight shed attained in this country, for all the talk of the great shed at Thornaby.....

Bottom right: Full circle. Kirkby has now disappeared of course, as if it had never been, but this picture of 23rd May 1970 has some historical piquancy. The new shed remains as a diesel depot (this served as part of the economic case for all these late sheds) whilst the old three road Midland building has been stripped and laid bare, retained only for its offices. The view is really startling, however, for the retention of the ash and coal plants (the photographer is standing on the latter) despite the closure to steam in about 1966. Surrounded incongruously by Type 1s, paired together as unlikely successors to the 8Fs (and 9Fs from the 1960s) the great concrete towers had seen barely eight years of use.

One of the Kirkby 8F fleet, No.48006, 5 July 1959. Photograph A.R. Goult.

Night and Day

Marvel with us at George Heiron's diurnal and nocturnal activities at Salisbury

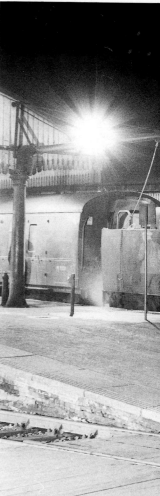

Bottom right. The wonders of the night. Battle of Britain Pacific No.34060 25 SQUADRON with an Exeter - Waterloo express is attended at Salisbury in 1961 - note the suitably ghostly engineman by the tender.

Top right. Tamed, diminished somehow by daylight, Merchant Navy Pacific HOLLAND-AFRIKA LINE at Salisbury, again Waterloo-bound.

Above. Back to the Night, and roaring safety valves fill the cold air as 35010 BLUE FUNNEL gets underway from Salisbury with a Waterloo to Exeter express in November 1962.

Ex-NER A8 4-6-2 tank No.69867 on the 1.55pm Whitby Town to Scarborough, climbing the last stretch of gradient to Ravenscar tunnel on a damp 13th July, 1957. Photograph Michael Mensing.

ALONG THE NORTH YORKSHIRE COAST

By 'MB'

Of all the railways that have disappeared during the last forty years, surely the coastal route from Teeside to Whitby and Scarborough must rank high in the scenery stakes. Hugging the coastline at several points on its journey, notably between Sandsend and Whitby, it provided spectacular views of the North Sea, and was a vital escape route from the gloom of industrial Middlesbrough, offering the summer pleasures of a holiday by the sea.

Built by two independent companies between 1875 and 1885, it was immediately taken under the wing of

Standard 4MT tank No.80120 waits to leave Ravenscar with the 4.20pm Whitby Town to Scarborough, 13th July 1957. Arriving (with the 4.27pm Scarborough to Middlesbrough) is B1 4-6-0 No.61037 JAIROU. Photograph Michael Mensing.

L1 tank No.67766 with the 9.7am Middlesbrough - Whitby Town, crossing Newholm Beck Viaduct, Sandsend, 16th July 1957. Photograph Michael Mensing.

the North Eastern Railway whose engineers soon discovered that the spindly viaducts dotted along its length were even more fragile then their appearance betokened. Instead of the planned concrete cores to the iron support tubes, the builders had filled them with loose aggregate and immediate (and costly) remedial measures

were need. The largest of these structures, north of Staithes station, spanned a very exposed and wind blown valley, so an anemometer wired to a bell was fitted, to warn if the crossing might be unsafe - no doubt with the recent Tay Bridge disaster in mind. In latter years the apparatus became unreliable and the tale is told

of a south bound passenger train one stormy night whose driver rang Staithes signalman to ask if the bell was ringing. Upon being told 'No!' His reply was 'it *!#*ing well should be!' and he hurtled across the viaduct with his cargo of humanity to such effect that he overran Staithes station and had to reverse.

A8 4-6-2T No.69867 makes a laboured progress up the gradient off Larpool Viaduct, 19th July 1957, with the 8.24am Stockton on Tees to Scarborough. Photograph Michael Mensing.

<table>
<tr><td colspan="5" align="center">**Scarborough 1st August 1954**</td></tr>
<tr><td>**Arrive**</td><td>**Origin**</td><td>**Loco**</td><td colspan="2">**Originating Departure Time**</td></tr>
</table>

Arrive	Origin	Loco	Originating Departure Time
A M			
11.22[R]	Bishop Auckland	77011	7.55
11.37	Darlington	77014	8.42
11.56[R]	Middlesbrough	67638	9.25
PM			
12.20	West Hartlepool	43055	9.10
12.56	Middlesbrough	43074	10.35
1.16	Stockton	69839	10.37
1.33 [R]	Middlesbrough	69852	11.08
1.51	Middlesbrough	43073	11.15
3.19	Stockton	61214	12.25
3.58	Scenic (Hull)	61010	
4.52	Whitby Town	69830	(return of 10.57am)
8.59	Whitby Town*	69885	(return of 2.20pm)

Depart	Destination	Loco	
A M			
10.57	Whitby Town	69885**	
PM			
2.20	Whitby Town	69839***	
5.00	Middlesbrough	43073	
5.33	Stockton	61214	
6.03	Middlesbrough	43074	
6.18[R]	Middlesbrough	67638	
6.33	Darlington	77011	
6.44[R]	Middlesbrough	69852	
7.03	West Hartlepool	43055	
7.33[R]	Darlington	77014	
8.03	Stockton	69830	

[R] = Relief Train

*passes 7.03 WH at Pros Hill, passes 7.33 [R] at RHB, passes 8.03 St. at Ravenscar.
**passes 11.22[R] at Cloughton, passes 11.37 D at Staintondale, passes 11.56 [R] at R'scar,
passes 12.20 WH at RHB, passes 12.56 M at WWC.
***passes 3.19 St at R'scar, probably passes Scenic at RHB.

RHB - Robin Hoods Bay
WWC - Whitby West Cliff
R'scar - Ravenscar
St - Stockton
D - Darlington
WH - West Hartlepool

This was a railway built mainly for passenger traffic; mostly a single line, there were passing loops at the larger stations. Whitby was served by a high level station at West Cliff, and a connecting steeply graded line led down to Whitby Town station. Odd trains did divert en route from Middlesbrough to Scarborough or vice versa but most called only at West Cliff. In the 1930s a Sentinel railcar spent its days shuffling between the two stations but latterly it was mainly trains starting or finishing at Whitby Town, and covering the section south to Scarborough, that used the line. Passengers from Teeside who did not have a connection employed local taxis to convey them and their luggage into town.

Traffic along the line was reasonably heavy in summer months and though, understandably, it was sparse at other times, it reached its peak in the pre-war years from 1933, when planners had the bright idea of changing the northern terminus from Saltburn to Middlesbrough. It really took off after this move, to such a degree that to ease congestion along the coast in the 1937 summer it was necessary for one holiday train non-stop from Middlesbrough to Scarborough to travel via Northallerton, Pilmoor, Gilling and Moulton.

Maximum line occupation was evident as late as summer 1954. While weekdays saw a steady flow of trains in each direction, the Sunday traffic was the busiest. A sequence of trains would follow each other south from Teeside to Scarboro' in the mornings, returning north from 5pm onwards. In effect the railway ran a system of one-way traffic.

The fly in the ointment however was the need to provide a basic service between Scarborough and Whitby Town. Two trains ran out of Scarborough at 10.57am and 2.20pm, returning from Whitby Town at 3.45pm and 7.42pm. The second train out of Scarboro' had an uneventful journey as most of the south bound trains had arrived, but the 10.47am had a difficult passage. The accompanying table of workings over the line on August Bank Holiday Sunday 1954 shows not only the six scheduled south-bound trains but also three reliefs; additionally a path was needed for a south bound scenic excursion between Whitby and Scarborough. This particular train originated at Hull, reaching Whitby via Driffield, Moulton, Pickering and Newtondale (now the track of the preserved North Yorkshire Moors Railway); similar trains ran on summer Sundays from several West Riding towns and cities. There were also two returning locals Scarborough - Whitby. On this particular day, one of them, the 10.57am ex-Scarborough, had to pass *five* trains before reaching Whitby Town so its timekeeping must have been poor. Locomotives working over the line in BR days comprised Gresley V1 and V3 tanks, Thompson L1s, ex-NER A8 4-6-2Ts, Robinson/Gresley A5/2s, LMR 4MT 2-6-0s and 2-6-4Ts and three types of BR Standard, 3MT 2-6-0, 3MT 2-6-2 tank and 4MT 2-6-4 tank (the highly successful 80000 class). Scenic excursions were hauled usually by B1s and an occasional class 5 whilst Scarboro's clutch of D49s ventured as far north at Whitby.

The line north of Whitby West Cliff closed completely on May 3rd 1958 - due in part to the deterioration of the viaducts and the southern section to Scarborough (latterly served by dmus) followed in 1965.

Today the track bed between Whitby West Cliff and Boulby (where the new potash mine is rail served) has largely disappeared. The viaducts were quickly dismantled and the formation has been reclaimed to a large extent. Southwards from Whitby West Cliff it remains intact, used as a long distance footpath. Indeed plans have recently been announced to lay a 2ft steam-worked line over the path of the railway between West Cliff and Robin Hood's Bay, crossing over the magnificent Larpool Viaduct - the only major structure on the old railway to survive, for it was built of brick. If this venture succeeds, travellers will once again have the chance to gaze through a train window at the unforgettable coastline of North Yorkshire.

Right. Standard 4MT tank No.80117 arriving with the 4.20pm Whitby Town - Scarborough at Ravenscar on 15th July 1957 - note the 1 in 39 gradient to the north. Photograph Michael Mensing.

An Ivatt Mogul, No.43072, crosses the Larpool Viaduct at Whitby (lines to Town going down to right) on 19th July 1957. Photograph Michael Mensing.

The railway still runs through Loftus, en route to the Boulby potash mine. The station closed long ago but the main building still survives. A8 4-6-2T No.69880 arrives on a Scarboro' - Middlesbro' train. Photograph Neville Stead Collection.

Northbound departure from Staithes. The memorial cross is still in position today. Photograph Neville Stead Collection.

Not all the stations had passing loops. Hayburn Wyke, south of Ravenscar, is almost lost in a woodland setting and was nowhere near any village or town of that name - Hayburn Wyke was a nearby bay! Photograph K. Hoole, Neville Stead Collection.

43050 entering Sandsend station en route to Middlesbrough. Sandsend Viaduct is under the train, East Row hidden round the curve to the right and Newburn Beck Viaduct just visible above the fourth coach. Photograph K. Hoole, Neville Stead Collection.

Scenic excursion from Leeds, heading south up Ravenscar bank behind B1 61237, assisted by 3MT tank No.82029. The ferocious climb, at 1 in 39, was a severe test for the locos and slipping was commonplace. Robin Hood's Bay lays in the background. Photograph K. Hoole, Neville Stead Collection.

Whitby West Cliff station out of season. Two coaches sufficed for this train from Middlesbrough. Photograph Neville Stead Collection.

Far left. A Middlesbrough L1 stands at Staithes station with a southbound train. A camping coach stands on the left - a 1938 LNER Guidebook prices a week in such accommodation at three guineas! Photograph Lance Brown, Neville Stead Collection.

Below. Robin Hood's Bay station. 80117 takes a breather before tackling the climb south to Ravenscar summit. Photograph T.G. Hepburn, Neville Stead Collection.

Left. Mogul 43074, northbound out of Whitby, crosses East Row Viaduct and heads for Sandsend. Note the group of donkeys on the beach below. Photograph K. Hoole, Neville Stead Collection.

Into (and out of) the Murk...
A Celebration of Birmingham Snow Hill

MICHAEL MENSING was brought up within sight of the Leamington - Birmingham main line, about three-quarters of a mile from Solihull station..... *'During and after the War, like so many others, we were not a car-owning family, so we naturally used the fairly frequent local train service from Solihull, mostly into Birmingham which, being only seven miles away, tended to overshadow our lives. Thither my father travelled to work six days a week, and my mother would take me and my brother there fairly often for shopping. "One and two halves,*

Snow Hill return" was the request at the booking office and this reflected the fact that in those days all the Leamington line trains went into Snow Hill; Moor Street station reserved to itself the Stratford-on-Avon service.

'Some time in the early 1950s, well before the Modernisation Plan, the Western Region improved the frequency and regularity of the suburban services around Birmingham. The standard, symmetrical Great Western four-coach sets, which had been almost universal, were broken up into three coach sets with some

new BR Standard suburban ones mixed in, thus making more trains available. Generally, then, the Leamington trains served Moor Street station while the ones starting or terminating at Knowle & Dorridge remained loyal to Snow Hill. When dieselisation came in 1957 this pattern was maintained but the intermediate trains turned round at Lapworth, the next station out, and they also continued beyond Birmingham - an 'all stations' service from Lapworth through to Wellington.

'That is the background to my acquaintance with Snow Hill as it was. When I started work in 1949 on the north side of Birmingham I had to commute daily, Saturdays included, to Snow Hill and then by bus a couple of miles so I saw quite a lot in passing. I was not a very intense enthusiast - certainly not one of the shed-bashing brigade - and I didn't start photography until 1955. By 1957 I had a good enough camera to be fairly confident of reliable results and I used to take it to work quite often and get a handful of pictures at Snow Hill, either by a quick bus ride during my lunch hour or while passing through during the lighter evenings.

'In 1958 my place of work moved to South Yardley, on the east side of Birmingham, so my visits to Snow Hill became much less frequent. I still used the trains as far as Acock's Green so I kept very much in touch with the main Leamington route, but Snow Hill was much less available, firstly because the trains*

6009 KING CHARLES II on the 9.25am Aberystwyth - Paddington, leaving Snow Hill on 25th July 1959. Photograph Michael Mensing.

4986 ASTON HALL, its outline etched, almost, against the lingering steam and smoke, enters the tunnel at the south end with an up freight, 28th June 1957. Photograph Michael Mensing.

Hall 4-6-0 No.6929 WHORLTON HALL with a Birkenhead - Bournemouth (possibly relief or extra) leaving Snow Hill on 5th August 1961, at 1.03pm. Photograph Michael Mensing.

through a rigorous ticket inspection! It therefore became a place to take photographs mostly on Saturday afternoons and summer evenings, when journey arrangements made it convenient. On the other hand, New Street was always handy, so inevitably I took far more photographs there. Unfortunately, though, freight was almost unknown at New

often served Moor Street and secondly, because there was no access to the platforms at Snow Hill without passing

Street, whereas the GW route was always busy with a great variety of such trains passing through.

'When I started driving a car in 1963, I'm afraid Snow Hill saw very, very few visits by me; along with most other stations, I'm ashamed to say!'

2-8-2T No.7247 with up iron ore empties, waiting for signals on the through road in Birmingham Snow Hill, Sunday 25th September 1960. Photograph Michael Mensing.

Bottom left: 5100 2-6-2 tank No.5174 disappears off Platform 12 with a special all stations to Earlswood Lakes, for a Jazz Festival, on 8th July 1961. Photograph Michael Mensing.

Far right: 57XX pannier tank No.9724 proudly bursts forth with a down freight, coming out of the tunnel to enter Snow Hill on 30th July 1960. Photograph Michael Mensing.

Right: Modified Hall No.7912 LITTLE LINFORD HALL at Snow Hill Platform 7 with the 9.50am ex-Cardiff (General) via Hereford, 12th June 1957. Photograph Michael Mensing.

THE END OF THE LINE
PENZANCE

Railway Station & Eastern Promenade, Penzance.

Wot.....no Combined Volumes? The view of Penzance station from the Promenade was - and still is - something of an observer's dream, but in this view the two lads seem more entertained by the photographer than the comings and goings beneath the wall. Assuming that this picture was taken in the Edwardian era, a chap with a huge tripod-mounted camera would indeed have had a novelty value. Despite the sunshine, the interior of the station, under the timber roof, has an air of unwelcoming gloom - this changed little until parts of the roof were dispensed with, albeit very gradually, many years later.

In the eyes of all true Cornish folk, the River Tamar at the eastern end of their county marks the border with the foreign land known as England. The people of Cornwall are fiercely independent, and the farther west one goes, the greater the feeling of independence. Consequently, when the railways first arrived in West Cornwall they were viewed, not as a means to help visitors to arrive but, instead, as something which enabled the locals to travel abroad.

The first public passenger railway in West Cornwall was the Hayle Railway, which opened its first stretch of line - between Portreath and Hayle - in December 1837, although scheduled passenger services were not actually inaugurated until 1843. For a short while it remained a localised concern, albeit a fairly successful one; the town of Hayle itself was, at that time, the main port for the handling of locally-mined copper, and business in and around the town was good. The first real hint that the Hayle Railway might become less parochial came in 1844, when the West Cornwall Railway was promoted with two principal intentions - firstly, to take over and upgrade the Hayle Railway (circumventing the two rope-worked inclines) and, secondly, to extend it to Truro (in the east) and Penzance (in the west).

The WCR's first Bill was rejected, mainly on the grounds that

the district deserved a better scheme than that proposed. It was, perhaps, not entirely coincidental that the original scheme had been the brainchild of the WCR engineer, Captain Moorsom, who, despite an obvious lack of adequate experience, had held important engineering positions with at least two major railway companies. It was widely considered that Moorsom had landed these positions through a combination of bluff (on his part) and a naiveté on the part of his employers. Furthermore, rather than hire experienced assistants or take sound advice, Moorsom had invariably insisted on going it alone. The rejection of Moorsom's scheme for the WCR was yet another failure to add to his lengthy list - indeed, it was said that Moorsom had taken more bills to Parliament than any other engineer, and had lost all but one of them. On the West Cornwall Railway, Moorsom was 'moved upstairs' in 1847 to make way for a new engineer - Brunel.

In his revised plans for the WCR, Brunel, somewhat predictably, opted for the broad gauge, principally with a view to a connection, at a future date, with the Cornwall Railway and the great beyond. The revised scheme received Royal Assent in August 1846, but before long the WCR found its coffers embarrassingly empty and so, to help reduce the cost of building the proposed line, standard gauge was adopted instead. There

was, however, a rider in the revision clause - the WCR was required to make the works wide enough to accommodate the broad gauge, and to lay broad gauge rails on six months notice being given by a connecting broad gauge company.

Early days

Construction of the WCR finally commenced in 1851. The line was laid with Barlow rails, which started to arrive by sea at Penzance in late October 1851 - this was, incidentally, the first time Brunel had used such rails. It seems that the engineering work was undertaken at a fair old pace, as the line was presented for the obligatory inspection on 8th and 9th March 1852.

The inspecting officer, Capt. Laffan, reported that the line: '.....now leaves Penzance, passes through Marazion, St.Earth [sic] and Hayle, and about three miles from Hayle, joins the rails of the old line [the Hayle Railway] .....the material in the cuttings and embankment is excellent, consisting generally of gravel shale and white rock, and in the case of the embankments sometimes of mine refuse.....the cutting at the entrance to the Penzance Station is exposed to the washing of a heavy sea; it is protected by a sea wall built of granite 18 feet in height and 6 feet thick at the bottom and 3' 6" at top - set in Aberthaw lime.....' Capt. Laffan was satisfied, and recommended that the new line be opened for public traffic. The first public services ran on 11 March (1852). At the eastern end of the WCR, the extension of the main line through to Redruth was opened on 25 August 1852. Two days later, the West Briton and Cornwall Advertiser reported that the first through train from Redruth to Penzance: '....was propelled by three engines, and had forty waggons crammed with passengers....' . Unfortunately, neither of the above mentioned reports made specific reference to the railway station at Penzance. The initial public passenger service between Penzance and Redruth comprised three trains each way on weekdays and two on Sundays, with a third-class single fare of 1s 4d.

The WCR's adoption of Barlow rails proved to be a false economy, as derailments (partly due to the method of ballasting, it must be said) became commonplace. In 1861 a start was made on replacing the Barlow with Vignoles rails, laid on longitudinal timbers, but the following year it was decided to lay double-headed rails. While this was going on, the Cornwall Railway - which had opened its main line from Plymouth to Truro in May 1859 - was trying to

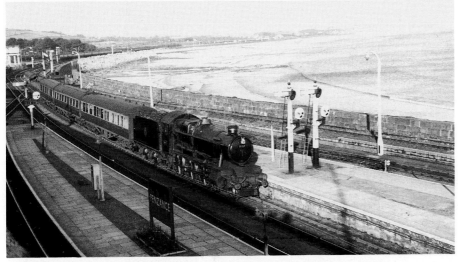

No.1007 COUNTY OF BRECKNOCK, in commendable condition, brings the 4.25pm from Truro into Penzance on 26 September 1956. The double island platform layout at Penzance station was created during the rebuilding of the late 1930s. Photograph H.C. Casserley.

enforce its right to have the WCR provide the third rail so that broad gauge trains could work through to Penzance. The WCR was in no hurry to oblige - the company was making a modest profit, but the work would involve an outlay it could ill-afford. The outcome was that, in 1865, the WCR sold out to an associated committee which represented the GWR, the Bristol & Exeter and the South Devon, and after a six-month changeover during which the 'big three' jointly worked the WCR, the official take-over was on 1 January 1866.

Under the new administration, work was soon put in hand to lay the third rail between Truro and Penzance. The work was inspected for the Board of Trade by Col. Yolland in October 1866, but was declared 'incomplete' - it was 1 March 1867 before it was finally opened to public passenger traffic. The broad gauge,

No.1007 was allocated to Truro from January 1955 until September 1959 and inevitably during that period, appeared regularly at Penzance. This, perhaps, narrows down the date of the picture. In the distance, Penzance Signalbox is discernible - this was opened in April 1938 to replace an older 'box a little to the east. Photograph J. Davenport.

however, lasted only until May 1892, after which it was standard gauge only, not just at Penzance, but also on the whole of the GWR network.

Penzance Station

The original passenger terminus at Penzance had two platforms and, seemingly, a complete lack of run-round or engine release facilities. A centre road was added by 1880, and a second centre road by 1893, but it appears that neither of those extra roads could be used for running round. The original terminus proved woefully inadequate,

TABLE ONE:
PENZANCE STATION - PASSENGER TRAIN TRAFFIC

	Staff		Receipts	Tickets		R'cpts	Parcels	
	No.	Wages £	Total £	Issued	Season	£	No.	R'cpts £
1903	52	5,279	52,324	122,555	-	18,131	317,783	34,193
1913	55	6,138	34,700	140,395	-	26,225	195,100	8,475
1923	57	11,443	105,112	137,335	430	37,524	360,787	67,588
1929	56	11,169	84,818	98,628	467	37,055	317,474	47,763
1930	59	11,189	85,330	87,682	747	34,607	332,622	50,723
1931	59	11,982	87,517	82,224	1,130	30,852	362,388	56,665
1932	59	12,202	79,178	78,692	1,694	29,889	334,596	49,289
1933	60	12,293	81,447	81,638	1,880	29,261	355,681	52,186
1934	60	13,068	82,128	83,813	2,394	30,626	349,748	51,502
1935	70	14,376	75,301	80,639	2,425	31,289	313,164	44,012
1936	72	15,718	79,690	76,852	2,361	32,103	343,207	47,587
1937	77	16,241	75,443	75,218	2,622	33,598	325,812	41,845
1938	78	17,095	77,430	66,595	2,585	33,245	332,661	44,185

After the rebuilding of Penzance station in the late 1930s, it was the usual practice for the 'Postal' (the Penzance-Paddington TPO) to use Platform Four as that provided the most convenient access for GPO vehicles. This picture was taken on 6 September 1956. Photograph Eric Sawford.

especially after the introduction of through broad gauge trains in 1866, and improvement work undertaken in 1879/80 was not really a permanent solution. These efforts were formally inspected for the BoT by Major Marindin in October 1880 - '....the buildings provide very good accommodation,

and the platforms are under a roof. The points and signals have been interlocked and are worked from a new cabin containing 22 levers of which 2 are at present spare....' A later inspection - in March 1907, referring to a new crossover between the up and down lines - stated that Penzance signalbox then had 36

levers, all in use. The original 'box, incidentally, was extended in 1893 but closed *circa* 1912, being replaced by a new 42-lever 'box slightly to the east.

For many years, especially during the early 1900s, plans to enlarge the cramped station were constantly thwarted by Penzance Town

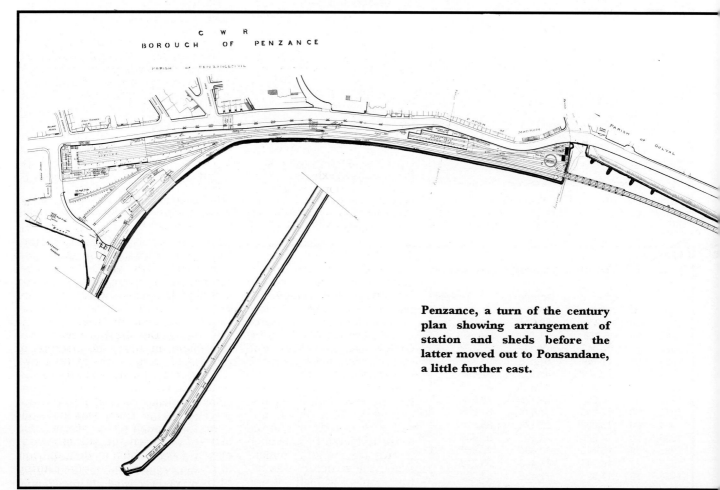

Penzance, a turn of the century plan showing arrangement of station and sheds before the latter moved out to Ponsandane, a little further east.

Council. The state of play was such that, at peak times, it was occasionally necessary to start trains from St.Erth station as space simply wasn't available at Penzance. It was 1931 before even a modest improvement was made at Penzance, and this took the form of an extension to the platform on the south side of the station. However, significant improvements were not far off as, between 1937 and 1940, the whole place was re-modelled. The improvements were

TABLE TWO
PENZANCE - GOODS TRAIN TRAFFIC

| | Staff | | R'cpts | FORWARDED (TONS) | | | RECEIVED (TONS) | | | | |
	No.	Wages £	Total £	Coal/coke	Other min's	General goods	Coal/coke	Other min's	General goods	Total (tons)	L'stck (vans)
1903	?	?	46,448	1,705	203	20,076	240	1,652	20,239	44,121	659
1913	18	1,285	40,552	1,420	703	12,412	980	4,988	26,260	47,690	764
1923	19	3,480	86,263	568	1,347	12,194	3,795	3,368	24,501	52,297	742
1929	28	4,899	77,000	214	1,138	9,423	3,297	5,639	23,544	45,945	912
1930	27	4,953	76,272	-	880	9,382	1,901	4,197	23,559	43,642	901
1931	27	4,907	74,144	293	1,017	8,268	970	4,523	23,585	40,412	937
1932	27	4,800	69,907	596	505	9,195	910	3,043	20,750	36,626	928
1933	26	4,935	69,983	448	720	10,444	543	3,540	19,158	35,986	821
1934	28	5,242	83,387	452	755	14,457	609	4,995	22,289	45,092	920
1935	28	5,679	82,711	137	509	12,427	1,251	3,809	24,113	42,987	1,099
1936	28	5,629	87,915	-	755	13,132	1,021	4,938	27,693	48,442	1,143
1937	29	6,014	92,125	-	864	14,796	753	6,491	31,442	55,621	624
1938	34	7,889	125,857	9	746	27,190	1,117	5,062	35,490	71,431	691

* Figures for 1938 include traffic handled at Marazion. During each of the previous two years, some 14,600 tons of goods traffic had been handled at Marazion for receipts of £27,000.

partly enabled by the removal of the goods depot from the station yard to Ponsandane (q.v.). A twin-platform format was retained, but both were now double-sided platforms, thus providing a total of four platform faces. The works were completed in September 1940. In 1944 the northernmost road (Platform One) was lengthened, and in its new form extended almost up to the terminal wall. Another aspect of the general improvements of the period was the provision of a new 75-lever signalbox (brought into use on 24 April 1938) and the construction of a new sea wall on the south side of the station area.

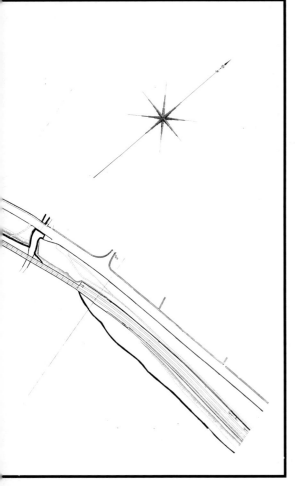

Part of the site of the old goods yard was subsequently given over to carriage accommodation, although over the years space for additional stock was found between Penzance and Marazion. The siding which extended beyond the old goods shed along Albert Quay was subject to a Private Siding Agreement (original PSA. dated 29 April 1849) with Penzance Town Council and later Penzance Corporation, but the siding was realigned in 1926 and later fell into disuse. It was, however, reinstated in August 1949 for a PSA with Western Salvaging Co. (later Penzance Shippers & Salvage); that agreement was terminated in March 1959 and the siding was disconnected soon afterwards.

Despite the remodelling of Penzance station in the 1930s the old overall timber roof was retained, though the end gables were finally dispensed with in the mid-1950s. The retention of the roof itself has actually presented a problem in recent times, as HST sets have to stop short for reasons of exhaust extraction. The station was partially remodelled in 1980, and in 1982/83 the passenger and staff facilities were improved.

Penzance Viaduct
One of the principal features of the railway approach to Penzance was the long, low timber viaduct. *(A lengthy article about the viaduct appeared in the June 1922 issue of the GWR Magazine - beware of alleged 'original' text in recent articles and books!).* The original viaduct was 347yd long and had no less than 51 spans, averaging 19ft in length, and with a clear width of 12ft 6in at the rail level. Despite such impressive-sounding dimensions, the structure was actually only 12ft high - it was

stated to be the *lowest* railway viaduct in Cornwall. Mysteriously, Capt. Laffan's inspection report (dated 10 March 1852) referred to the timber having been 'Burnettized' - a process intended to help preserve the timber by treating it with a solution of zinc chloride - but a later report referred to the timbers having been 'Kyanised' - a different form of preservation, named after its creator, Dr John Kyan (1774-1850) which involved pickling the wood in dichloride of mercury. Whichever treatment the timbers actually received, both forms had, since the 1840s, started to fall from favour as the use of creosote had become more widespread.

The original viaduct did not remain intact for very long. On 27 December 1852 - only nine months or so after the line across it had opened - the structure was severely damaged during a heavy storm, which coincided with a period of spring tides. The viaduct was rebuilt, but on 24 January 1869 was partially destroyed by another storm. One of the main problems, as explained in the *GWR Magazine* article, was that the floor of the viaduct was close-decked, and so there was no exit route for the sometimes vast amounts of water and shingle hurled up by heavy seas. That flaw was rectified when the viaduct was rebuilt, the decking of the new structure being punctuated by 'wide open spaces'. While the viaduct was being reconstructed a temporary line was laid slightly inland - it was not until 28 October 1871 that the 'new' structure was brought into use.

Despite the revised design - and, in 1895, the insertion of rolled steel joists - the viaduct had to be constantly monitored. As explained in the *GWR Magazine*, an ongoing problem - possibly not fully appreciated at the time it was first built - was that much of the viaduct was believed to be on the site of a submerged forest, which made it difficult to obtain a solid foundation. During the rebuilding work of 1867-72 it was

By 11 May 1959 - when this picture was taken - the timber gable ends of the station roof had been removed, thereby making the interior of the terminus somewhat less dark and gloomy. No.4955 PLASPOWER HALL has recently arrived at Platform One with the 7.35am from Newton Abbot. Photograph Michael Mensing.

possible to replace only nine of the timber piles by masonry piers, the lack of solid foundations requiring the retention of timber piles elsewhere in the structure.

As the years progressed, the viaduct became an increasing hindrance to the handling and development of traffic at Penzance - the line across the viaduct was only single track, and at times it created a considerable bottle-neck. Furthermore, by the twentieth century the weights of some of the new locomotive types were perilously close to the limit the

viaduct could accommodate. The solution, announced in 1920, was to replace the viaduct with an embankment, which would effectively double as a breakwater.

The new embankment, built on the site of the viaduct and laid with a double track, was completed in July 1921. Railway traffic had not been interrupted. The embankment was granite faced, and had a 3ft high parapet on the seaward side. At the extreme western end of the wall were three openings - a 6ft span over a sewer, a segmental arch of 11ft span

over a stream, and an 18ft span girder bridge giving access to the beach. Near the eastern end of the wall, the Ponsandane River had an outlet to the sea under an 11ft span arch.

A dome too far....
On 30 November 1878, the boiler of broad gauge 0-6-0ST IAGO exploded at Penzance station - '.....the dome of the Iago engine, which was attached to the 3.50pm passenger train [five passenger coaches and a brake] was blown off just as the train was going to start for Plymouth. No persons were hurt, but the cast-iron dome in which the safety valves are seated, and the brass cover, were blown into the air, came down through the roofs of the station, and of a passenger carriage that was standing in the siding under the station roof, and lodged on the floor of the carriage. A small piece of brass dome cover fell on the public road, about 80 yards further off, and a piece of the wood cleading was picked up on the sea beach at the south side of the railway'. The official report was very detailed, and it included an interesting snippet about the locomotive's recent working life - it had been sent to the South Devon district from Swindon at the beginning of February 1877, and had been used at Exeter as a shunting engine. It had been repaired at Newton Abbot, entering the works on 24 March 1878 and returning to traffic on 30 October, and had been dispatched to Penzance on 11 November.

At that time, the engine shed at Penzance was a twin-road structure on the north side of the running line just to the east of the sta-

The empty stock of the 7.35am from Newton Abbot is backed out of Penzance by the train engine, No.4955 PLASPOWER HALL. The date is 12 May 1959 - the day after the other photo of the same engine on the same working. The obvious inference is that the engine was on a regular diagram that week. Photograph Michael Mensing.

TABLE THREE:
PENZANCE STATION - PASSENGER TRAIN TRAFFIC

	Staff No.	Tickets Issued	Season	R'cpts £	Parcels & milk No.	R'cpts £	Other R'cpts £	Total Receipts £
1953	151	86,453	3,018	80,380	577,627	89,220	1,793	171,393
1954	148	90,759	3,352	78,622	333,340	85,836	1,844	166,302
1955	151	86,956	3,004	77,779	213,914	81,647	1,688	161,114
1956	149	92,536	3,239	83,340	291,828	96,559	1,780	181,679
1957	151	103,543	3,735	92,237	453,733	97,547	2,012	191,794
1958	149	97,421	2,931	91,759	425,130	72,021	2,179	165,959
1959	150	94,774	2,599	97,364	358,828	75,172	2,223	174,739

days, when washouts etc. had been attended to.

Another episode relating to the old engine facility at Penzance was rather tragic. GWR Locomotive and Stores Committee minute, 20 January 1897: *'GEORGE CROWLE, cleaner, 1s/6d per day, injured Penzance 3rd and 5th November 1896. On 3rd November Crowle was assisting to coal an engine, and in order to raise the coal tub slightly, he went to the handle of the crane and appears to*

The 1.55pm Penzance-Plymouth, headed by No.6875 HINDFORD GRANGE, passes Long Rock engine shed on 11 May 1959. In the distance, behind the rear carriages of the train, can be seen the roof of Ponsandane Goods Depot, which was built in 1937 to replace the cramped goods facilities alongside the passenger terminus. Photograph Michael Mensing.

tion - that shed had been built in 1876 to replace a very small one on a nearby site. The shed foreman, a Mr John Ivey, was interviewed in connection with the IAGO incident, and his remarks give a brief, but interesting, glimpse of operations at the shed. He stated that IAGO had arrived at Penzance on the night of 11 November, working the 6.10pm passenger train from Ply-

mouth. The engine had, on that day, replaced PLATO (a similar 0-6-0ST), which the driver had worked to Plymouth with the 11.15am passenger train from Penzance. Since 11 November, IAGO had been regularly used on the 11.15am mixed train from Penzance to Plymouth, returning with the 6.10pm passenger - the engine's usual stoppage day had been Thurs-

have removed the pawl of the ratchet wheel, causing the handle to fly round and strike him between the eyes, both of which were made purple. Crowle did not leave off work, and two days after, while engaged cleaning out the firebox of an engine, his foot slipped and the pricker which he held pierced his eyelid and entered the eyeball, completely destroying the sight'. The parents of the unfortunate lad subsequently applied to the GWR for financial assistance, but were told that the best that could be done was to 'get Crowle elected to a blind asylum'. His parents refused, stating that they were not willing to let him leave home. A later investigation by the GWR centred on the ratchet and pawl which had been involved in the first accident, and although the report was inconclusive, the somewhat heartless bottom line - indicative, perhaps, of the 'master and servant' employment ethos of those days - was that the second accident (i.e. that which resulted in Crowle being blinded in one eye) would have had the same outcome even if the first accident had not occurred.

A train of empty stock from Penzance passes Long Rock (the shed is partly hidden by the coal stage) on 11 May 1959. The engine is No.1005 COUNTY OF DEVON of Bath Road - it actually spent all of its working life based in Bristol, transferring in 1960 to St.Philips Marsh from where it was withdrawn in 1963. Photograph Michael Mensing.

To return to the subject of the Penzance shed itself, the original depot was alongside the goods shed on the south side of the station. In July 1876 a new twin-road engine shed

TABLE FOUR:
PENZANCE STATION - MILK TRAFFIC FORWARDED, 1950s
Receipts figures included in parcels figures in Table Three

	Gallons	Cans	Cases	Tanks	Receipts £
1953	1,548,103	161	94	729	26,049
1954	1,325,439	107	-	730	25,621
1955	1,445,701	-	98	719	29,674
1956	1,611,661	-	95	662	34,260
1957	1,865,802	-	111	697	38,155
1958	1,267,016	-	117	437	23,257
1959	1,555,260	-	71	573	26,864

was opened just to the east of the station on the north side of the running line (almost opposite the ticket platform, which remained operational - nominally, at least - until the end of 1901), and the original premises were incorporated in the 'new' goods shed. In 1914 a new engine shed opened at Ponsandane, a mile to the east, and the old shed near the station was subsequently demolished, some of the stone being used - so the story goes - in the new embankment, built in 1921. The story of Ponsandane shed is beyond the remit of this modest article, but has been covered recently in *BRILL 5.6, March 1996.*

Passenger and Tourist Traffic

Prior to the 1890s the tourist traffic in West Cornwall was negligible, but in the thirty years between 1890 and 1910 passenger traffic in the county virtually trebled. The GWR was not slow to respond to the increase in tourism, nor to develop year-round local traffic. In October 1903 the company introduced a motor bus service between Penzance and Marazion - this was only a little over two months after its much publicised introduction of the bus service between Helston and The Lizard. Two more motor bus services were added in 1904 - Penzance-Lands End in April and Penzance-St. Just in May. By 1910, those three bus services from Penzance involved eight vehicles.

As for ordinary passenger services, in the 1880s the fastest through trains to and from London took 9hr 15min down and 8hr 55min up. In July 1901 a new 7hr 52min service from Paddington - 'The Cornishman' - was introduced, and by the late 1920s it was possible to travel from Paddington to Penzance in 6hr 20min.

Passenger transportation on the GWR was revolutionised in 1892 when corridor trains were introduced, although it was June 1893 before they first appeared on the Penzance route. In July 1904 the GWR introduced the '10.30 Limited' - better known in later years as the 'Cornish Riviera Express' - and in 1935 (the GWR's Centenary year) the train was provided with new purpose built rolling stock - the carriages 60ft long and 9ft 7in wide, and a thirteen-coach formation could seat 84 first- and 336 second-class passengers, with dining car accommodation for a further 88. Another title - 'The Cornishman' - was reintroduced in the summer of 1952 and applied to the daily train to/from Wolverhampton while, on 28 January 1957, the title of 'The Royal Duchy' was bestowed on the existing 11am Penzance-Paddington and 1.30pm Paddington-Penzance services.

Of the other services, one worth noting is Penzance-Aberdeen - 785 miles in about 21 hours - which was introduced in 1901. Another important service was the 'Postal' - the TPO - which was inaugurated between Paddington and Penzance in January 1902. After Penzance station was rebuilt in the late 1930s, the usual practice was for the 'Postal' to use Platform Four, as that provided the most convenient access for GPO vehicles.

Goods Traffic

The original goods depot at Penzance was on the south side of the passenger terminus. It was destroyed by fire early in 1876, and its replacement - on the same site - incorporated the old engine shed, which was 'tacked on' to the north-west wall of the goods shed. By the early 1920s it was handling over 50,000 tons of goods each year, and although that figure dropped during the Depression of the late 1920s and early 1930s, by the mid-1930s the figure was increasing towards the 50,000-ton mark once again. Somewhat inevitably, conditions were, by then, extremely cramped.

Some three-quarters of the goods traffic handled at Penzance was categorised as 'general merchandise'. One of the important outgoing commodities was broccoli, and by the 1930s over 26,000 tons of the stuff was dispatched by rail from Cornwall (al-

Billed as "the last steam working to Penzance", the RCTS/Plymouth Railway Circle special of 3 May 1964 was hauled from Plymouth by No.34002 SALISBURY. This was the first and last time a Bulleid Pacific had reached Penzance. Alterations to the roof have lightened the age-old gloom. Photograph Hugh Ballantyne.

The RCTS/PRC special of 3 May 1964 waits to depart from Penzance. For GWR traditionalists agonising over this sight, a slight diversion is offered by the view of the old goods yard - compare this with earlier photos to see how things had changed since the mid-1930s. Photograph Hugh Ballantyne.

beit not only from Penzance) each season. During the peak month of April well over 230 special broccoli trains were usually run from Cornwall, and by 1934 the GWR was able to boast that over 2,000 truck loads were dispatched in one week. There were other garden produce - notably flowers, which bloomed early in West Cornwall due to the milder climate. That said, the earliest flowers of the season came from the Isles of Scilly, but were shipped to Penzance for onward transportation. During the 1930s over 1,000 tons of flowers were brought from the Scillies each season, most of them by rail to Covent Garden in London or to various provincial markets.

Another regular commodity exported by rail from Penzance was fish, especially pilchards. The local fishing trade was vital to the community, but on various occasions the usually reliable pilchard - such a dependable little creature - had almost disappeared from the Cornish coasts, much to the detriment of the local economy. This was, perhaps, most notable in the 1870s, when a prolonged dearth of pilchards coincided with a severe downturn in the Cornish mining industry. Fortunes in the county were extremely poor, and it was to be at least a couple of decades before any relief was available in the form of tourism.

But the fish *did* return to Cornwall. And they returned in enough numbers to warrant an article in the company's in-house publicity organ, the *GWR Magazine*. The October 1935 issue of that magazine included an enthralling sounding feature entitled *The Pilchard - A Notable Cornish Visitor*. The magazine - which blew the corpo-

rate trumpet at every opportunity - proclaimed that: *'The pilchard rarely visits any but Great Western territory, and consequently "goes Great Western" when it is finally caught and barrelled'*. A fish with a preferred mode of transport? By the time that article was written the main fishing port in West Cornwall was Newlyn, which had grown in stature during the late 1800s - at the expense of several smaller ports - largely because of its proximity to the 'new' rail head at Penzance. Newlyn continued to prosper, and by the 1930s it handled almost 60% of all fish landed at West Country ports. By that time, incidentally, the once busy fishing port of St. Ives handled a mere 3% of West Country catches.

By the mid-1930s the traffic in broccoli, flowers, pilchards and various other types of merchandise handled at Penzance was such that new goods facilities were desperately needed. Indeed, the old premises had been in need of replacement for some considerable time, but the availability of financial assistance from the Government - in the forms of the Loans and Guarantees Act, which was intended to encourage major civil engineering projects, thus combating unemployment - provided the catalyst. The GWR might have been a very proud company, but Government assistance wasn't to be sneered at.

In 1936 it was decided to relocate the goods department to new purpose-built premises at Ponsandane, about a mile or so east of the passenger station. The new depot was completed in 1937, and the goods department formally transferred to its new home on 1 December of that year. The new depot comprised a 280ft-

long single road goods shed, a warehouse with some 400sq yd of floor space, a yard with two mileage sidings, each holding some 60 wagons, and siding accommodation for a further 50 wagons.

Locomotives and Workings

The only GWR locomotives officially prohibited from working through to Penzance were the Kings and the 47XX 2-8-0s. The restriction was, in fact, on those engines crossing the Royal Albert Bridge between Plymouth and Saltash, but although a King is known to have appeared in Cornwall on at least one occasion, none of the class ever got as far as Penzance.

The heavy passenger trains to and from Penzance, which had once been handled by the GWR's distinctive double-framed 4-4-0s, were, by the early 1930s, usually worked by 4-6-0s. The two most important workings at Penzance were probably the 'Riviera' and the 'Postal', and although Penzance shed usually had at least one Castle on its books, principally for one or other of those important trains, it was far from uncommon for Granges to be given the 'Riviera' and, on a slightly less frequent basis, for Halls to work the 'Postal'. Until the emergence of the Castles, incidentally, the 'Postal' had usually been worked by an Exeter-based Star. The Castles which appeared at Penzance were by no means all West Country engines; taking two examples at random, in November 1957 two Old Oak Castles were observed at Penzance on consecutive days - No.5082 departing with the 2.00pm parcels on 13 November (having arrived earlier that day with the down 'Postal') and No.7030

Above. The 22.10 sleeper for Paddington awaits departure from Penzance on 1 August 1975 behind Class 52 No.1068 WESTERN RELIANCE. Photograph Brian Morrison.

Below. A fine telephoto view of Penzance terminus on 7 July 1976, with class 45/0 No.45028 waiting to depart with the 18.00 to Sheffield. Photograph Brian Morrison.

on 14 November with a Royal train conveying the Duke of Edinburgh.

Until the 1930s a significant proportion of native mixed traffic locomotives had been 83XX 2-6-0s - the modified versions of the 43XXs - but Hall and, later, Grange class 4-6-0s gradually moved in to take over the majority of main line workings. It was actually the Granges which came to dominate, the quota of locally-based examples gradually increasing over the years so that, by early 1958, no less than twelve were allocated to Penzance shed. Nevertheless, despite the growing ranks of Granges at Penzance and, from the mid- and late 1940s, a gradual, if small, influx of County and Manor 4-6-0s, the Halls were never completely ousted from 'the end of the line' - far from it. During the BR era, other locomotives regularly stationed at Penzance included a Castle or two, 43XX 2-6-0s, the ubiquitous pannier tanks and a modest handful of 2-6-2Ts (45XXs and, earlier, 44XXs), principally for the St. Ives and Helston branches. The public timetable for the summer of 1955 showed that, on Sundays, two of the St. Ives branch trains (in each direction) worked through to or from Penzance - today, throughout the week most DMU services on that branch work right through to/from Penzance.

As for non-GWR locomotive types, probably the first 'foreigners' to be seen at Penzance with any regularity were the LMS 8Fs. During the war, the dispersal of 8Fs was such that one, LMS No.8435 (a Swindon-built example), was actually allocated to Penzance shed from new in 1944, principally for the broccoli traffic. In the BR era, Standard Pacifics were first seen in Penzance on 28 August 1951 when Britannia No.70019 worked the 'Riviera' between Plymouth and Penzance. A regular diagram for the Britannias stationed at Laira in Plymouth took in the 4.50am Plymouth-Penzance, 9.45am Penzance-Plymouth (the up 'Riviera' - presumably the engines were changed near Laira shed), 3.05pm Plymouth-Penzance (the down 'Riviera' - again, engine changing near Laira), and the 7.30pm Penzance-Plymouth, a total of 320 miles daily.

Conventional locomotive workings were disrupted whenever the Penzance turntable was out of action. This occurred in the autumn of 1935 and again in autumn 1945. Rather than have locomotives running tender-first to and from Truro (26 miles away - the location of the nearest 'table), additional tank engines were transferred to Penzance for the duration. For the 1945 hiatus, various large 2-6-2Ts were drafted in to work passenger trains on the Truro-Penzance section, while 2-8-0Ts and 2-8-2Ts looked after the heaviest freights.

The next (and, as it turned out, final) major overhaul of the Penzance 'table took place in May/June 1956. This time, sixteen 51XX 2-6-2Ts and two 61XXs were transferred temporarily to Truro and Penzance sheds for working the main line trains between those two points. Those drafted to Penzance were Nos.4107, 4114, 4148, 5107, 5161 and 5184 although, of those, No.4107 spent most of the time in the repair shop, with No.4134 (temporarily attached to Truro) for company. The 51XXs often struggled with the heavier loadings, especially the 8.45pm up sleeper, and were therefore tried double headed with that train. Even that failed to cure the problem and so, until the Penzance 'table was back in action, a Castle was subsequently sent light to Penzance - tender first - each evening to take charge of the sleeper. For the heaviest goods workings, a Hall (No.4908) and two Granges (Nos.6800 and 6826) remained in use between Penzance and Truro, running tender first in the down direction.

Although the use of 51XXs on main line passenger trains at Penzance was a little out of the ordinary, it took a lot to startle local observers. This was especially true on summer Saturdays, when anything and everything could - and sometimes did - turn up with passenger trains. The use of 28XX class 2-8-0s on peak season passenger trains was far from unknown, but in 1956 No.3862 was turning up at Penzance with such regularity that somebody wrote to a railway magazine to query if the engine had been allocated to Penzance. It had not. That said, it should be emphasised that, although 28XXs appeared at Penzance regularly up to *circa* 1947 (almost invariably with freights), during the 1950s they were less frequent visitors.

In 1958 the first of the D600 and D800 series of Warship diesel hydraulics entered service on the West of England route, and although the D600 series engines were to prove embarrassingly unreliable, the D800s fulfilled most expectations. Initially, they were usually reserved for the Paddington-Plymouth section, but before long they became regular performers between Plymouth and Penzance. In contrast, the D600s spent part of their later lives working almost exclusively on the St.Blazey-Fowey line - presumably out of harm's way. For secondary duties, the Type 2 (D63XX series) diesel hydraulics gravitated towards Cornwall during 1959, and soon took over most of the remaining main line duties. In Cornwall they were often used in pairs, but the loadings of some trains were such that a steam locomotive - often a Manor 4-6-0 - was routinely rostered to pilot a pair of them, forming a spectacular triple header with the Manor at the front.

Steam traction lingered on at Penzance (albeit with increasing rarity value) until 1962, the engine shed at Ponsandane being offi-

---

PENZANCE STATION
Scheduled arrivals and departures of passenger services, summer Saturdays 1955 *N.B: Services shown in italics did not operate for the whole duration of the summer timetable.*

5.50am ex-Newcastle
6.05am ex-Paddington
6.30am ex-Paddington
7.30am to Wolverhampton
7.45am ex-Paddington (sleeper)
7.55am to Truro
8.20am to Paddington
8.25am ex-Wolverhampton
8.40am ex-Paddington (sleeper)
8.50am ex-Truro
9.05am ex-Paddington
9.50am ex-Plymouth
10.00am to Paddington *
10.05am to Liverpool
10.20am to Cardiff
10.45am to Sheffield
11.10am ex-Paddington
11.10am to Wolverhampton
11.30am ex-Manchester
11.50am ex-Plymouth
11.50am to Paddington
12.00   to Glasgow
1.20pm to Paddington
1.50pm ex-Liverpool
1.55pm to Newton Abbot
2.30pm ex-Plymouth
2.40pm ex-Paddington
2.50pm ex-Swindon
3.35pm to Truro
4.00pm ex-Bristol
4.10pm ex-Birmingham
4.20pm to Newton Abbot
4.25pm ex-Ealing Broadway +
4.40pm ex-Paddington
4.45pm to Manchester
5.00pm ex-Truro
5.25pm ex-Paddington *
5.40pm ex-Paddington
6.10pm to Truro
6.35pm ex-Truro
6.45pm ex-Wolverhampton
7.00pm ex-Paddington
7.05pm to Truro
7.05pm to Manchester
7.20pm to Plymouth
7.45pm ex-Paddington
8.10pm ex-Carmarthen
8.15pm to Paddington
8.25pm ex-Bristol
8.45pm to Paddington
8.55pm ex-Manchester
9.30pm ex-Liverpool
9.30pm to Paddington (sleeper)
9.55pm ex-Paddington
10.00pm to St.Austell
10.55pm ex-Paddington
* Cornish Riviera Express
+ Until 25 June and after 27 August, started from Paddington.

---

cially closed to steam in September of that year. The turntable survived until 1964. Somewhat ironically, the last steam working at Penzance - or so it was thought - was on 3 May 1964 when an RCTS/Plymouth Railway Circle special was hauled by Bulleid Pacific No.34002 SALISBURY - a blow for GWR traditionalists! Another irony was that this was the *first* time a Bulleid Pacific had visited Penzance. Isambard would not have been amused.

Acknowledgements:
Some details of the station layout at Penzance were gleaned from *Track Layout Diagrams of the Great Western Railway* by R.A. Cooke. General advice and assistance was kindly provided by Messrs. Maurice Dart, Eric Youldon and Bryan Wilson, to whom considerable thanks are due.

FOURUM

Above: The Welsh Highland Railway (Light Railway) Company, to give it its full and unwieldy title, never attained the same national (global?) celebrity status as its neighbour, the Festiniog Railway, despite the fact that the two concerns were very similar in character, their 1ft 11.5in gauge lines negotiating, as they did, the 'vast slate amphitheatre' of North-west Wales. In corporate and operational terms, the WHR and the FR had much in common, culminating in 1934 in the FR leasing the WHR. The West Highland ultimately extended from Dinas Junction (on the LNWR south of Caernarvon) to Portmadoc, though the southern section of the line wasn't completed until 1923. One of the stations on that new section was at Beddgelert, 14 miles south of Dinas Junction. In this photograph, the freshness of the works, captured for a commercial postcard, seems to indicate a date soon after the opening.

Below: Beddgelert station again. The locomotive is Hunslet 2-6-2T RUSSELL, which had been built for the Portmadoc, Beddgelert & South Snowdon Railway (one of the WHR's two constituent companies) in 1906. On passing to the WHR, RUSSELL was cut down in size so that, in theory, it could work over the lines of the Festiniog but, in practice, an adequate reduction in width proved impossible. RUSSELL survives today, having been restored to working order by the Festiniog Railway preservation group.

Above: The WHR's second locomotive was Vulcan Foundry 0-6-4T MOEL TRYFAN, which was inherited from the other constituent company, the North Wales Narrow Gauge Railway. Its erstwhile twin, SNOWDON RANGER, had been cannibalised *circa* 1917 to provide parts. As far as can be ascertained, the coaching stock seen here is part of the WHR's complement of 16 carriages - mostly bogie vehicles - which originated with the NWNGR.

Below: The WHR tried to capture a share of the local tourist business - its efforts extended to passenger trains slowing down through the Aberglaslyn Pass so that visitors could take in the view - but the tourist traffic failed to make a much needed difference to the corporate coffers. Despite the area's undoubted scenic delights, anybody promoting tourism in North Wales had (and still has) to play down the less than tropical weather - witness here the almost horizontal plume of smoke from RUSSELL's chimney, on what is seemingly a summer's day. Nevertheless, the WHR was bold enough to introduce a buffet car - it is seen here next to the locomotive. These days, narrow gauge railways are often dismissed as the playthings of preservationists - but such a dismissive attitude is quite out of order. Lines such as the Welsh Highland were proper working railways, serving the local communities and industries in a more suitable manner, maybe, than a dauntingly engineered - and disproportionately expensive - standard gauge line. And that, of course, assumes that it would have been physically possible to construct a standard gauge line in the first place. This little bout of pontification leads - in a foreseeable manner, perhaps - to positively the last unashamed plug for *RAILWAY BYLINES* magazine - a sort of 'Son of BRILL', published on alternate months by your very own Irwell Press. Narrow gauge railways are featured regularly in *RAILWAY BYLINES*, along with an intriguing mix of branch lines, minor railways and industrial lines - the sort of railways which are often ignored by the 'mainstream' railway press. How ever did we manage without it........?

Early Days

In Britain, there were several lengthy cross-country railways constructed through bleak and almost uninhabited terrain. So - why build a railway across extremely difficult territory when there was precious little local traffic for the taking? There were various reasons, one being what lay at the other end. In the case of the Dingwall & Skye Railway - almost sixty-four miles long, and much of it hugging the river valleys across the wonderfully empty countryside of what is now Ross & Cromarty - the main prize was the fish traffic from northwest Scotland and the Isle of Skye to the markets in the south. Additional prizes in the railway company's sights were sheep and cattle, and also the seasonal, but potentially important, tourist traffic.

The Dingwall & Skye Railway was a nominally independent concern, but it had £50,000 of back-

The Kyle Line

'...this being the first case of a railway passing through deer forests'.
By Martin Smith, Editor of Railway Bylines

45473 climbs away from Loch Luichart with the Inverness - Kyle mail, May 1961. Photograph Rail Archive Stephenson, W.J. Verden Anderson.

ing from the Highland Railway and £100,000-worth from the Caledonian. The Highland undertook to work and maintain the line for a period of ten years, the terms being 2s/0d per train mile for each of two daily trains each way, 1s/10d per train mile for any trains in excess of two each day, plus

a rent for the use of Dingwall station. At the end of the ten-year period, the railway was to be handed over 'in good order, ordinary wear and tear excepted'.

The construction of the Skye railway was not entirely straightforward. Initially, it was proposed to

route it via Strathpeffer - a newly-fashionable spa resort and, therefore, a potentially useful source of traffic - but local landowners, in particular Sir William Mackenzie, objected to the projected route and the railway company was forced to adopt a new alignment a couple of miles to the north. This de-

One can always tell when it's summertime at the Kyle of Lochalsh - the drizzle can be quite warm. It's 28 July 1953, and the 9.05am ex-Inverness has just arrived. Photograph Brian Morrison.

viation was via Raven's Rock, 458ft above sea level and on a four-mile long ascent of 1 in 50. It was not the easiest obstacle for a railway to negotiate. Strathpeffer *did* become rail-connected, but not until 3 June 1885 when a 2.5 mile branch from Fodderty Junction, a couple of miles or so west of Dingwall, on the Skye line, was opened.

Another major problem - albeit not a physical one - facing the construction of the Skye railway was the potentially huge cost of the final

ten-mile section between Strome Ferry and the Kyle of Lochalsh, but that financial obstacle was circumvented by truncating the line temporarily (at least) at Strome Ferry, where a timber pier was built. The 'temporary' status of Strome Ferry as a terminus was to last for twenty-seven years, despite the hazardous currents in Loch Carron which could cause severe problems for shipping.

The railway between Dingwall and Strome Ferry - 53 miles instead of the projected 63° miles to

the Kyle - was opened to goods traffic on 5 August 1870. Permission to open to passengers had been denied by the

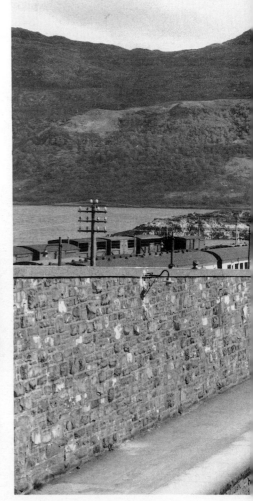

During the 1950s (and maybe beyond) a couple of former Caley 2P 0-4-4Ts were outstationed at the Kyle of Lochalsh (at least in summer) for shunting/piloting. On 28 July 1953, No.55216 was on duty. Photograph Brian Morrison.

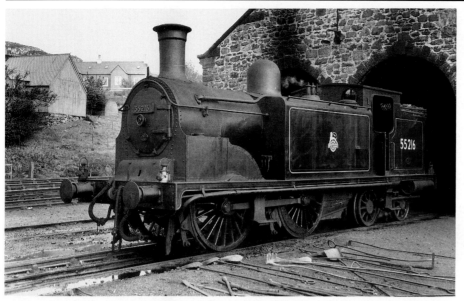

A fine study of Kyle pilot No.55216, on shed on 3 May 1957. Photograph Hugh Ballantyne.

Board of Trade inspector, Capt Tyler, who had carried out a thorough inspection of the line between 28 July and 2 August and had reinspected on 8 August. The BoT report commented that the line was: '...an interesting example of economical work in the case of a line constructed at the expense of landed proprietors and others interested in the district through which it runs, but on which the traffic can never be expected to be very heavy. With a view to economy, steep gradients, and in some cases, sharp curves have been adopted.

'...this being the nature of the line,

and it is being intended by the Company to run mixed trains only of goods and passengers over it, I have thought it right to strongly recommend that the total time for running between Dingwall and Strome Ferry should not in the first instance be less than three hours...it is quite probable that the company may, after a time, see their way to safely increasing that speed when the Engine drivers and guards have become thoroughly acquainted with the line and when continuous breaks have been brought into use for the safer working of the trains'.

Capt Tyler reported that a total of 11 miles of the line was on a gradient of 1 in 50, while a further 31° miles was at 1 in 100 or steeper. The sharpest curve had a radius of only 9° chains (and was 11 chains long) while a total of 29 curves had a radius of 15 chains or less. Four of the curves were fitted with check rails. The customary description of the works noted the use of double-headed rails weighing 70lb per yard and in lengths of 24ft, chairs weighing 26lb, transverse sleepers of Strathspey Fir, ballast of nine inch-thick gravel, and fencing of wire for much of the route but with wooden 'bars' where the line passed through the deer forests on Glen Carron and Achnashellach estates — '...this being the first case of a railway passing through deer forests'. It was noted that there was only one overbridge on the entire line, but there were numerous underbridges and viaducts variously constructed of masonry, timber, wrought iron and cast iron. The largest span of any of the structures was 130ft — '...lattice wrought iron on masonry piers...' — which carried the railway across the River Carron near Strathcarron. The summit of the line, incidentally, was at Luib, 646ft above sea level.

During his inspection, Capt Tyler noted various requirements:

'At the Dingwall Junction, certain trees to be cut down or lopped, by which the view of the signals, either from the

Could this be the most scenic railway location in Britain? Mercifully, the monstrous new road bridge to Skye (at the time of writing - February 1996 - protesting Islanders are being piped into court) won't obscure this particular view - but how on earth was permission for any sort of bridge granted in the first place? The date is 3 May 1957, and No.45179 stands at the platform with the 5.40pm to Dingwall and Inverness. Photograph Hugh Ballantyne.

One for cash-strapped modellers - Glencarron station which, until 10 September 1962, had officially been titled Glencarron Platform. It was photographed on 4 July 1967 - some three and a half years after closure on 7 December 1964 - and it clearly hadn't been neglected. Was there a reason for the continuing maintenance of the closed station? Photograph Michael Mensing.

signalmen or from approaching Engine Drivers was obscured...at Grudie Falls, where the slope had been partly washed away by a torrent (this was August, after all!), the longitudinal timber placed for greater security under the cross sleepers to be extended; certain portions of rock are being removed to prevent a recurrence of this mischief ...the cast iron girders at Altmore (21° miles) not appearing to be trustworthy, to be replaced by others...on the cliffs at Loch Carron, to cut down all trees which might possibly be blown over on the railway in a gale, and examine and roll down all loose stones...the sudden change of gradient from 1 in 50, east of Frenchman's Burn to be eased off...improved signal arrangements and locking apparatus at Strome Ferry...landing stage required on the pier for the convenient and safe landing of passengers at different periods of the tide...'

A BoT inspection report often sounded fairly disastrous - a bit like a surveyor's report on an old house - but for the railway companies things were rarely as bad as they first sounded. This was largely true of Capt Tyler's report, most of the requirements being relatively straightforward, although the condition of the fencing was considered so unsatisfactory that opening to passenger traffic was denied.

The down 'Hebridean', hauled by Type 2 (later Class 26) D5339, passes Glencarron station on 4 July 1967. Photograph Michael Mensing.

On 6 July 1967, D5067 (later designated Class 24) arrives at Achnashellach with the down 'Hebridean'. The loop (serving the up platform) at the station had been removed in March 1966. Photograph Michael Mensing.

Capt Tyler reinspected the line on 18 August (1870), and this time he was satisfied enough to recommend that the line be sanctioned for public passenger traffic. There were, however, a few matters to clear up: '...At Dingwall, a means of shelter is much required, especially on the arrival platforms from the Skye line and from the north at this station...it is desirable that a system of bogies, or of Engines and Carriages otherwise adapted for sharp curves,* should be prepared for use on this railway, not only for greater safety but also economy of haulage and of wear and tear to permanent way and of rolling stock...'.

Public passenger traffic on the Dingwall-Strome Ferry line commenced on 19 August 1870, and on the same day steamer services were inaugurated between Strome Ferry and Portree on the Isle of Skye and to Stornoway on the Isle of Lewis. The new railway, although not ideal in every respect, provided the islanders, in particular, with a vastly improved means of communication with the outside world. But not everybody was happy with the new railway.

Trouble at t'pier
Before very long, the most vociferous objections to the railway were being raised by the Free Church of Scotland - the 'Wee Free' - whose ministers and

During the 1960s, one of the redundant 'Devon Belle' observation saloons was resuscitated for use on summer season trains on the Kyle line. Here, it is attached to the down 'Hebridean' leaving Achnashellach station. The date is 6 July 1967. Photograph Michael Mensing.

Strathcarron station typifies the simple but pleasing (and invariably well maintained) stations on the Kyle line. A down freight, hauled by D5127, restarts from Strathcarron on 6 July 1967. Photograph Michael Mensing.

parishioners took great offence to the off-loading and onward transportation of fish from Strome Ferry on the Sabbath. The railway company took little heed of the protests, replying that fish caught in the Minches or beyond on a Friday evening or Saturday morning, and cured at Stornoway, would arrive at Strome Ferry late on the Saturday evening or early Sunday morning, and have to be dispatched immediately in order to reach the London markets first thing on Monday. Indeed, the railway company was under an obligation to the Stornoway curers to provide such a service.

Matters came to a head on Sunday 3 June 1883 - fairly early in that year's herring season - when a crowd of Sabbatarians gathered at Strome Ferry, principally to prevent work being undertaken on the Sabbath, such work obviously including the unloading of vessels. The crowd gradually grew in number to over one hundred men, many of whom were armed with sticks, and their mood became increasingly hostile. The railway company employees - a mere twenty or so in number - tried to continue working as best they could, but were eventually forced to stop by the mob. The stationmaster at Strome Ferry watched the incident, and telegraphed

the night superintendent at Inverness station to say that, unless the police were dispatched to Strome Ferry promptly, the mob looked like remaining in possession of the pier until Mon-

day morning. Only eight policemen could be mustered at such short notice (the entire Ross-shire Constabulary comprised only 36 men) and, inevitably, their attempts to enforce law

The 5.30pm Kyle of Lochalsh-Inverness, hauled by D5335 and with the ex-'Devon Belle' observation car at the rear, about half a mile north of the Kyle. The date is 7 July 1965. Photograph Michael Mensing.

On 7 July 1965 Type 2 D5335 leaves the Kyle of Lochalsh behind, having departed with the 5.30pm to Inverness. Photograph Michael Mensing.

and order against a crowd which, by that time, had grown to 150 or more were futile. The mob, having succeeded in halting work on the Sabbath, gradually adopted a less aggressive stance, and immediately after midnight (i.e. at the beginning of the Monday) started to disperse.

The incident generated intense controversy. One school of thought was reported in the *Ross-shire Journal*: '...the Highland Railway being held by many "to be the shabbiest corporation extant"'. An opposing view appeared in the *Northern Chronicle*: '...the trucking of fish is, after all, a more seemly employment on a Sunday morning than fighting with police'. While the debate continued, the Sabbatarians made it known that they intended to stage a repeat performance the following Sunday but, to the relief of the authorities, no confrontation ensued. That, however, was not the end of the matter. Ten of the participants in the riot of 3 June were subsequently arrested and tried on charges of mobbing, rioting, assault and breach of the peace, and after being found guilty each was sentenced to four months imprisonment - a sentence which, in the opinion of many, was far too harsh. However, public opinion eventually won the day and the

men were released before half their sentences had been served. As for the railway, the HR subsequently had relatively trouble-free, if not uncontroversial, Sunday workings at Strome Ferry. (A comprehensive account of the riot and the politics which surrounded it is given in *The Strome Ferry Railway Riot of 1883* by David McConnell , published by Dornoch Press, 1993).

On to the Kyle

The original intention of extending the railway to the Kyle of Lochalsh seemed to be conveniently forgotten, but in 1889 authorisation was granted for the construction of the potentially competitive West Highland Railway to Fort William, and there was already talk of extending that unbuilt line to Mallaig, from where the Isle of Skye and the Outer Hebrides could be served by boat. The threat of a possible rival jolted the Highland Railway into reluc-

tant action, and in June 1893 it obtained powers for a 10.5 mile extension from Strome Ferry to the Kyle of Lochalsh, complete with a pier at the latter point. The extension was difficult to build, no less than thirty-one cuttings having to be excavated, mostly through solid rock, and twenty-nine bridges constructed, but despite the intensity of the works the extension was ready for opening on 2 November 1897. The new facilities at the Kyle rendered the pier at Strome Ferry redundant, and it closed simultaneously with the opening of the extension. The old pier at Strome Ferry nevertheless remained in situ until 1937, when it was demolished by the LMSR.

It is useful here to take a look at the Dingwall-Kyle of Lochalsh line as a whole. It was single track and had passing places at most of the intermediate stations, outline details of the various stations, sidings etc (in-

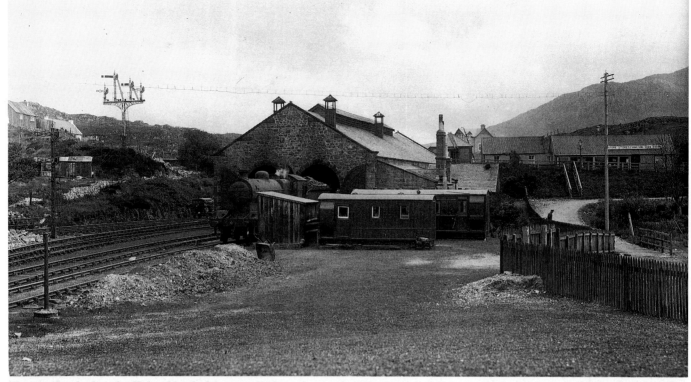

The engine shed at the Kyle of Lochalsh was a little to the north of the station. The structure, which opened with the extension from Strome Ferry in 1897, was solid-looking and displayed the Highland Railway penchant for a separate arched entrance to each road. This view, dating from June 1936, shows Cumming 4-6-0 No.17953 outside the shed. Note the well-maintained nature of things - the yard in the foreground is bereft of clutter, and even the old coach bodies have clearly benefited from a recent lick of paint. Photograph R.M. Casserley Collection.

cluding later installations) being:

Fodderty Junction (2m 22ch from Dingwall) - not a stopping place, but an important landmark on the line as it was the point at which the Strathpeffer branch (opened in June 1885) diverged.

Fodderty Timber Siding (approx. 2m 30ch) - opened February 1913 and closed by December 1915; presumably used to help transportation of timber during World War I.

Achterneed station (4m 53ch) - allegedly opened with the line in August

1870, although original BoT inspection report made no mention of 'Strathpeffer' station, as it was titled until 1 June 1885. Had second platform on passing loop and short goods siding at west end.

Raven's Rock Siding (some 25ch west of Raven's Rock summit) - opened 1925 to serve a stone crushing plant which supplied 'road metal for the Cromarty County Council'. The BoT inspection report, dated 13 July 1925, noted that '...the sidings have not yet been brought into use as the crushing

plant is not ready.....it is desired to work traffic from the direction of Dingwall and this will necessitate a loaded train leaving the sidings with the engine at the higher end of the train....trains should be limited to five loaded wagons with a 16-ton brake van and the connection used during hours of daylight only'.

Tarvie - private siding on down side of line opened *circa* 1914.

Garve station (11m 69ch) - opened with the line in 1870. Small goods yard on south side of station.

Lochluichart station (*approx* 17 miles) - originally a private station serving Lochluichart Lodge, relocated and converted for public use (complete with a new siding, installed at Lady Ashburton's expense) on 1 July 1871. It was relocated for a second time on 3 May 1954 when the line was deviated for the construction of a new reservoir. The deviation added a distance of 2 chains to the line, and this should be taken into account with the remainder of the stations etc. Extract from the Appendix to the Highland Railway WTT for 1920: *'When Mixed trains have to shunt at Lochluichart the Guard or Brakesman must attend to the working of Points from Ground Frame while the Stationmaster is engaged with the collection of Tickets'.*

Achanalt station (21m 40ch) - opened with the line; originally spelt as 'Achanault'.

Achnasheen station (27m 70ch) - opened with the line; spelt 'Achen Nasheen' in BoT inspection report. Goods sidings on north side of line. The Appendix to the Highland Railway WTT noted that: *'All Trains to be allowed*

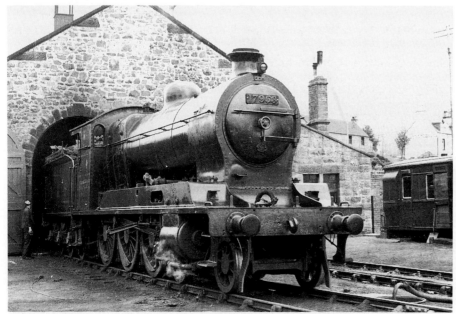

Cumming Superheated Goods 4-6-0 No.17953 poses at the Kyle of Lochalsh on 18 June 1937. The engine was withdrawn in September 1948 without having had its BR number (57953) applied. This picture was taken on 18 June 1937 - some nine years after the class had commenced their successful residency on the Kyle line. Photograph H.C. Casserley.

The railways approach to the Kyle of Lochalsh and the site for the turntable required the removal of a considerable quantity of rock - the requisite works can be clearly seen in this photograph, which is dated 1913. A splendid period piece..... Photograph R.M. Casserley Collection.

three minutes at Achnasheen. Orders for Luncheon or Tea Baskets to be accepted by Guards and Stations, and transmitted to Achnasheen by telegraph free'.

Achnasheen Ballast Pit Siding - opened *circa* 1903 for railway use.

Loan Siding (34m 10ch) - opened July 1914.

Glencarron platform (36m 18ch) -

added on 1 August 1873. HR Appendix 1920: *'All Ordinary Trains to stop either by signal or notice given at Achnasheen or Achnashellach Stations, as the case may be....Mailbags (for which trains will only slow) between Glencarron and Achnasheen twopence (2d) each'.*

Achnashellach station (40m 32ch) - opened with the line, albeit officially a

private station (with a siding) until circa 1871, when it became 'public'. Loop and second platform added 1900. Highland WTT Appendix: *'In working the Traffic at this Station particular care should be taken to leave no portion of a Train standing on the gradient of 1 in 70 on the Kyle side of the Station while Shunting is going on, unless the Engine is at the Kyle end of such a portion'.*

1936, and Cumming 'Superheated Goods' 4-6-0 No.17955 (later - albeit fairly briefly - BR No.57955) approaches the Kyle of Lochalsh with the down 'Lewisman'. Photograph R.M. Casserley Collection.

The Jones Skye Bogies were purpose-built for the Kyle line and, as a class, spent the majority of their lives on that line until displaced by the Superheated Goods 4-6-0s in the late 1920s. This magnificent view shows Skye Bogie No.14279 (ex-HR No.86, built in 1893) shunting at the Kyle on 20 June 1927. Note the engine's Jones-style louvred chimney, albeit with a Drummond-style flared top. Photograph H.C. Casserley.

Strathcarron station (45m 69ch) - opened with the line. Two platforms; goods facilities on north side.

Attadale station (48m 15ch) - added 1 March 1878. Single platform; one siding plus shunting neck. WTT Appendix dated 1920 notes that: 'The station has been temporarily closed for Traffic, but Trains will continue to call at the Platform to take up and set down Passengers as at present'. The same Appendix (1920) noted that the single fares from Attadale to Strathcarron (2.5 miles) were 4d first and 2d third-class, and to Strome Ferry (5 miles) 9d first-class.

Strome Ferry station (53m 8ch) - the original terminus. Originally had overall roof - although it covered precious little of the down platform! The roof was removed *circa* 1939/40. A twin-road engine shed, with access from a 43ft 7in turntable, was in use at Strome Ferry until the opening of the extension to the Kyle in 1897. The engine shed was demolished by 1904, if not long before.

Portachullin Ballast Siding - provided in August 1903.

Duncraig station (57m 2ch) - private platform serving the Duncraig Castle estate opened with the extension on 2 November 1897. The HR Appendix for 1920 noted: 'On Mr.Fletcher's personal application to either of the Stationmasters at Plockton or Stromeferry (sic), or to any of the Guards, to stop Trains at Duncraig

Platform - Mail Trains excepted - it must be done'. The platform finally became 'public' on May 1949.

Plockton station (58m 15ch) - opened with line. Single platform with goods sidings.

Duirinish station (59m 49ch) - opened with line. Closed temporarily 17 July 1915 to 1 January 1920. Single platform with no sidings, but nevertheless handled public goods (nominally, at least) until February 1954.

Kyle of Lochalsh (63m 52ch) - twin-faced platform on pier and extensive sidings. Engine shed to the north of the station adjacent to the running line - the site of the turntable was on land that had been hewn out of the rock. In typical Highland practice, the shed had a separate arched entrance to each of its two roads. The original turntable was 50ft in diameter, but in the 1940s this was found to be inadequate for the 'Black Fives' and so the LMSR installed a 54ft 'table - not a simple task as the additional space had to be blasted out of solid rock. The coal stage - little more than a platform, in fact - was later fitted with a corrugated iron shelter; nearby was a 21,000-gallon water tank.

Working the Line

When the extension to the Kyle of Lochalsh was opened in 1897, the services comprised two passenger, one mixed and one goods train each way on weekdays, most of the trains running through, to or from Inverness. A similar level of services prevailed for many years, usually including an early morning, a late morning and a late afternoon/early evening train in each direction. The regular 'all stations' trains between Dingwall and the Kyle

Achnashellach station, 18 June 1937. Cumming 4-6-0 No.17956, facing in the up direction, manoeuvres at the down end of the station. Do we see the letters 'GW' on a couple of the wagons? Note also the item of machinery on the down platform. Photograph H.C. Casserley.

The stations towards the north end of the Kyle line were not often photographed. Garve was typical; extremely neat and usually impeccably maintained. This picture, which was taken on 21 July 1931, faces towards Dingwall. Photograph H.C. Casserley.

were gradually accelerated over the years, from around 3 hours 30 minutes at the turn of the century to around three hours by the 1950s, but there were various expresses to grace the public timetables from time to time, usually during the summer.

Having mentioned summer season expresses there were, in fact, two year-round trains which were christened by the LMSR. One was the 'Hebridean' and the other the 'Lewisman', and both were timed to connect with steamer sailings - by MacBraynes, of course - to and from the Kyle of Lochalsh. As has been documented elsewhere, for some years it was normal practice for the down 'Lewisman' to have its restaurant car detached at Achnasheen, where the trains crossed, and placed on the up 'Hebridean'. Another named train, the short-lived 'Strathpeffer Spa Express', which operated from 1911 to 1913 only, negotiated the eastern extremity of the Kyle line on its journey between Aviemore and Strathpeffer.

By the summer of 1952 the public timetables listed the following:
Down: 9.05am ex-Inverness, 9.55am at Dingwall, thence just three regular stops (plus request stop to pick up at Achterneed and SO stop at Strome Ferry), arrive Kyle 12.28pm.
10.30am ex-Inverness, 11.18am at Dingwall, all stations, arriving at the Kyle at 1.59pm. This train carried the mails.
5.10pm ex-Inverness, 6.02pm at Dingwall, all stations (Glencarron by request or arrangement and Duncraig by request), arriving at the Kyle at 8.42pm.
Up: 5.05am ex-Kyle, non-stop to Dingwall arriving 7.16am, arr. Inver-

ness 8.01am. (28/6 to 4/9 only)
6.25am ex-Kyle, all stations (Duncraig and Glencarron by request only) to Dingwall arr.9.26am, arr. Inverness 10.22am. In the WTT this was listed as a mixed train.
10.45am ex-Kyle, all stations (Duncraig and Attadale by request only) to Dingwall arr.1.43pm, arr. Inverness 2.24am. This was the up mail train.
5.40pm ex-Kyle, all stations (Glencarron and Lochluichart by request only) to Dingwall arr.8.23pm, arr.Inverness 9.05pm.

It is interesting to note that, of the 1952 services, the 10.30am ex-Inverness

was advertised as having a restaurant car as far as Achnasheen, while the 10.45am from the Kyle of Lochalsh had a restaurant car from Achnasheen. Clearly, the practice of transferring the restaurant car from a down train to an up train at Achnasheen was perpetuated well after the days of the 'Lewisman' and the 'Hebridean' (and indeed continued until the early 1960s) although in 1952 the scheduled arrival of the down train at Achnasheen at 12.32pm meant a somewhat early (or hasty) lunch for passengers travelling to the Kyle. Another item of that 1952 timetable (albeit shown only in the relevant WTT) was that on Saturdays the 5.10pm ex-Inverness and the 10.45am

A little-known corner of Kyle engine shed.

Kyle shed in 1957 - the old LNW coach seems to have been put in for the convenience of enginemen working in on extended shifts during the Second World War.

ex-Kyle called at 'Imber House, Balnacra Level Crossing Gatehouse, Craig Houses and Luib Houses to take up or set down wives of Railway Employees'.

The conveyance of mails on Kyle line trains is an intriguing subject in itself; entertainingly covered by John Roake in the summer 1994 issue of the *Highland Railway Journal* - the magazine of the Highland Railway Society. It is impossible to do justice

to the matter in a modest article such as this; suffice it to say that in 1930 the LMSR put letter boxes on the trains on thirteen routes in Scotland, including the Kyle line. Initially, it was proposed that they would replace some of the local sub-post offices, but that proposal was soon dropped. It was decided that each letter box '.....*will be fitted into the window of the double door of the Guard's Brakevan and will have an additional posting slot in the box so that*

when the Van door is standing open letters may be posted in the Van from the platform'. The trains on which the letter boxes were used were the 10.10am ex-Inverness and the 4.50pm from the Kyle of Lochalsh - on the former the box did not prove to be particularly useful, but on the latter some 570 items were posted each week during the winter and 750 during the summer. The experiment was certainly successful, but the entire scheme

Kyle on a rare sunny day - seagulls reeling, an Austin *Ruby* on the platform and an Inverness Class 5 awaiting orders. Paradise Lost! Photograph T.G. Hepburn, Neville Stead Collection

Summer days meant increased traffic at Kyle; hence borrowed CR 0-4-4T No.55216 (a long term regular) with 60A (Inverness) shed plate, 8 August 1956. Photograph P.B. Booth, Neville Stead Collection.

came to a halt soon after the outbreak of war in 1939, never to be reinstated.

As regards goods traffic on the Kyle line, the mainstay was fish, but there was considerable diversification during both World Wars. In World War I the line was used extensively for military traffic from America, landed at the Kyle of Lochalsh, much of it for onward transportation to the naval bases at Inverness and Invergordon. The entire railway between the Kyle and Dingwall naturally

came under Government control during the war, and the Highland Railway was permitted to run only one daily train, for passengers and mails, each way on the line. It was a similar story during World War II, the railway again assuming strategic importance.

In peacetime, the railway to the Kyle and the ease of access from there to the Isle of Skye were well publicised. The *LMS Magazine* of March 1936, for example, included a stirring account of life on the Isle of Skye - the

'lonely misty isle' - emphasising that life on Skye had changed very little over the years, but the article also included a snippet of dubious usefulness to potential holidaymakers.... '*one thing...that is specially well done in Portree is the plumbing. There is a very good plumber in the town and though his materials are expensive, because they must travel two or three hundred miles before he gets them, he does his job exceedingly well'*. Just the sort of thing all tourists ought to know.

Kyle shed, bathed in sunshine; 45361 was a regular on the line. Photograph T.G. Hepburn, Neville Stead Collection.

Clan Goods No.57956 waits departure from Kyle with a lengthy train for Inverness date probably 1951 or 1952. Photograph Neville Stead Collection.

As already mentioned the working of the Kyle line was hindered by lengthy single-track sections, and although in peacetime the intensity of traffic wasn't usually enough to cause problems, local weather conditions could throw a spanner in the works. Indeed, it was possible for a train to leave Dingwall in brilliant sunshine but, by the time it reached Luib it could be struggling in a severe blizzard. Another problem was that of gradients, and arguably the greatest problems were encountered near Raven's Rock. The matter was addressed by the Ministry of Transport in July 1925, Lt-Col Mount reporting that: *'In connection with the operation of heavy down trains, both passenger and goods, upon the rising gradient between Dingwall and Raven's Rock summit, a bank en-*

Jones Goods No.17930 in from Inverness, stands outside Kyle shed accompanied by a large heap of ash and clinker - obviously the height of a pre-War summer - best guess is July/August 1935. Photograph Neville Stead Collection.

57956 shunting vans at Kyle, 28 July 1949. Photograph D. Butterfield, Neville Stead Collection.

pear to be desirable to attach the bank engine to the rear of the train at Dingwall (with vacuum pipes connected), uncoupling it at Achterneed before the train makes the ascent to the summit (thereby enabling the banker to 'drop away' after the train had passed the summit), instead of permitting the engine to run uncoupled as at present from Dingwall'.

Locomotives

The first regular locomotives on the Kyle line were 'Seafield' class 2-4-0s which had been built in 1858 for the Inverness & Aberdeen Junction Railway (one of the Highland's constituent companies). These locomotives were hardly ideal for such a challenging line, not least of all because of their rigid wheelbase, and in 1871 the HR's Locomotive Superintendent, David Jones, was granted authority to convert two of them to bogie 4-4-0s at a cost of £200 per engine. The two to be converted were No.7 and No.10, which were named DINGWALL and DUNCRAIG respectively following their conversion. It is thought that while No.10 was being rebuilt, it was fitted with what later became the standard Jones-style cab (prior to rebuilding, the two engines had nothing more than weatherboards to protect the crew).

The rebuilding of the two 'Seafields' was successful, and prompted the design of the celebrated 'Skye Bogies', the first of which, HR No.70, was completed at Lochgorm Works in 1882. Due mainly to the financial restraints imposed by the HR's directorate, construction of additional 'Skye Bogies' was extremely protracted - the second of the class was completed

gine is required. Apparatus has been installed at Achterneed, the station situated upon the gradient, whereby a special key is issued in respect of the bank engine in addition to the usual tablet for the Achterneed-Garve section, so *that this section may not be cleared until the bank engine has returned from the summit - which is situated between Achterneed and Garve - and the special key has been replaced in the instrument at Achterneed.... It would ap-*

Kyle on a dull day - 45361 with a train arrived from Inverness. Photograph T.G. Hepburn, Neville Stead Collection.

Kyle of Lochalsh as many have found it, with Skye capped by lowering clouds, and light levels at a minimum. An Inverness-bound train waits departure time. Photograph T.G. Hepburn, Neville Stead Collection.

in 1892 (ten years after the first) and by the end of 1901 (by which time the Kyle extension was operational) the total stood at nine. The later 'Skye Bogies' had longer tenders, and this necessitated a slight extension of the turntable at Dingwall. All nine of the class were to survive into LMSR days, the last to go being LMSR No.14284, withdrawn in 1930.

By around 1900 the 'Skye Bogies' had been augmented on the Kyle line by 'Strath' class 4-4-0s, but it was not until the withdrawal of the 'Skye Bogies' commenced in the 1920s that other types started to appear on the line with any real regularity. The newcomers during the 1920s were the 'Small Ben' 4-4-0s and, from 1928, the 'Superheated Goods' 4-6-0s, the latter type (alternatively known as the 'Clan Goods') gradually forging a strong association with the route. A 'Loch' 4-4-0 is known to have been tried on the Kyle line in the 1920s - the class had been prohibited north of Inverness prior to 1908 - while, during the 1940s (and possibly at other times) one was regularly used as the Raven's Rock banker. 'Jones Goods' 4-6-0s underwent trials on the Kyle line circa 1928, and it is believed that some of the class subsequently undertook the occa-

sional passenger duties - hopefully only during the summer periods as the locomotives were not equipped for train heating. During World War II, the 'Clan' class 4-6-0s started to appear on the Kyle line with reasonable regularity, and maintained a presence on the route until the class' extinction in 1952.

A visitor to the Kyle line in July 1945 reported in *The Railway Observer* that the remaining 'Clans' and 'Clan Goods' monopolised the line, with an occasional 'Ben'. Those noted were 'Clans' Nos.14764, 14767 and 14769, and 'Clan Goods' Nos.17950, 17954, 17955, 17956 and 17957, while No.14397 BEN-Y-GLOE was at Dingwall and No.14401 BEN VRACKIE at Kyle. A footnote added that '...the track is becoming weed infested in places and the running is none too smooth'.

It was some considerable time after the grouping before standard LMSR types started to be used on the Kyle line - partly a reflection of the line's 'specialised' motive power requirements and partly due to the weakness of some of the bridges, but also, perhaps, a reflection of the remoteness of the line from head office at Euston. The first real evidence of the LMSR regime

wasn't seen until as late as 1946, although it proved to be temporary. In 1946 seven Fairburn 2-6-4Ts were lent to Inverness shed by Polmadie while the Kyle of Lochalsh turntable was out of action, the engines usually working smokebox-first towards the Kyle and bunker-first towards Dingwall. The unavailability of the Kyle 'table was due to it being enlarged from 50ft to 54ft in readiness for the introduction of the 'Black Fives', various bridges on the line also being strengthened in preparation for the new machines. Somewhat inevitably, the 4-6-0s soon took over the majority of Kyle line duties, and by the end of 1952 had completely displaced traditional motive power. That said, a couple of former Caledonian 0-4-4Ts - for some time No.55216 and No.55237 - were outstationed at Kyle during the 1950s and 1960s for shunting and pilot duties. Another incomer to the line was one of the pair of former 'Devon Belle' observation cars which, as SC281, was customarily attached to the rear of trains during the summer seasons of the early and mid-1960s.

Changes Afoot

In 1961 'Type 2' (Class 26) diesels were introduced on the Kyle line, the plan

Type 2s Nos.D5334 and D5343 head away from Kyle of Lochalsh alongside Loch Carron, with the 5.30pm to Inverness on 6 September 1961 - former 'Devon belle' car at rear. Photograph Brian Stephenson, Rail Archive Stephenson.

Lovely view of Black 5 No.45124, with its big Scottish numbers, leaving the Kyle with an up goods around 1956. Steam blasting up out of the cutting has hit the air above and been dragged back by some natural effect, clinging and wreathing itself on the rock wall. Glorious! Photograph T.G. Hepburn, Rail Archive Stephenson.

45117 with the 10.45am Kyle to Inverness mail, crossing the River Bran soon after leaving Achanalt. May 1961. Photograph W.J. Anderson, Rail Archive Stephenson.

being for steam traction to be ousted by the start of that year's summer timetable. The diesel takeover went virtually to plan, and the last ordinary steam-hauled passenger working (other than specials) on the line was on 10 June. In the economy conscious years that followed, the future of the Kyle line came under regular scrutiny and, in 1971, closure was actually approved, albeit not until 1974 at the earliest. Ferocious opposition managed to secure a stay of execution but, unlike matters at countless other locations throughout Britain, the anti-closure lobby eventually won the day.

Somewhat ironically, the main weapon in the anti-closure armoury was the potential traffic to the Howard Doris construction site near Strome Ferry (where the master platform for the Ninian oil field was to be built), but although the line's reprieve was largely due to this factor (up to three or four goods trains each day being anticipated), the construction site closed unceremoniously in 1977. If nothing else, its brief existence helped to save the Kyle line although, most significantly, while closure was under discussion the traffic on the line actually increased by 100%. Good timing indeed!

Despite the line's escape from the axe, it did not totally escape cuts. For example, in December 1964 the stations at Achterneed and Glencarron were closed completely, while public goods facilities were withdrawn from the intermediate stations on the line during that same year. There were changes near the western end of the line in the late 1960s when the construction of a new road by-passing Strome Ferry necessitated the realignment of a section of the railway on to a purpose-built embankment on the shore of Loch Carron. Earlier, the new road had been perceived by some as a possible threat to the railway.

In 1983/84 the Kyle line made railway headlines when a system of two-way radio control was introduced. The new means of control enabled the removal of all conventional signalling and existing open wire communication circuits - a revision of operations which had been deemed necessary since the winter of 1978 when blizzards had destroyed most of the overhead pole and wire equipment in North-east Scotland, resulting in complete disruption of train services. The two-way radio system was generally successful, although it had taken extensive tests to pinpoint potential radio black-spots. Also, after the system was introduced it was found that the allotted radio frequencies interfered with emergency services - in Norway! A change of frequencies was required, and when this was eventually undertaken it was nec-essary to close the entire line for almost a month, during which a bus service substituted.

Nowadays, operations on the Kyle line are a far cry from what they used to be. Goods and parcels traffic has gone, Sprinters have replaced locomotive-hauled trains, and the transfer of the outer isles boat services to Ullapool has had an effect. But at least the line is still open. For some years now, it has been almost purely a tourist line - but a pretty spectacular one. The new road bridge across the water from the Kyle to Kyleakin might be a scenic disaster (to be fair, could any bridge blend in with the local landscape?) but the scenery along the rest of the route remains as magnificent as ever.

Sincere thanks to Mr Keith Fenwick of the Highland Railway Society for his assistance (sometimes from 30,000ft) during the preparation of this article. It should be noted that various issues of the Highland Railway Journal (the magazine of the Highland Railway Society) were consulted during the preparation of this article, while the extracts from the 1920 WTT Appendix are, in fact, taken from the Society's reprint.

45123 with an Inverness - Kyle train near Garve, 7 April 1961. Photograph D.M.C. Hepburne-Scott, Rail Archive Stephenson.

Black Five 45361 near Achanalt with a Kyle to Inverness train, 3 August 1960. Photograph D.M.C. Hepburne-Scott.